Stefan Kühl

Making use of Management Fashions

A Very Brief Introduction

AF173873

Springer

Stefan Kühl
Universität Bielefeld
Bielefeld, Germany

Competing Interests The author has no competing interests to declare that are relevant to the content of this manuscript.

ISBN 978-3-032-09264-9   ISBN 978-3-032-09265-6   (eBook)
https://doi.org/10.1007/978-3-032-09265-6

Translation: Previously published with SN

Translation from the German language edition: "Managementmoden nutzen" by Stefan Kühl, © Der/die Herausgeber bzw. der/die Autor(en), exklusiv lizenziert an Springer Fachmedien Wiesbaden GmbH, ein Teil von Springer Nature 2025. Published by Springer Fachmedien Wiesbaden. All Rights Reserved.

This Springer imprint is published by the registered company Springer Nature Switzerland AG.
The registered company address is: Gewerbestrasse 11, 6330 Cham, Switzerland

If disposing of this product, please recycle the paper.

Making use of Management Fashions

Preface

Management fashions invariably attract criticism. Economists complain that the proponents work with a simplistic understanding of organizations that has little to do with reality (for an early critique, see Hilmer and Donaldson 1996). As far as social scientists are concerned, many management books generate far more heat than light, while sociologists have decided that management fashions are as unavoidable as the annual flu virus: It only ever mutates slightly, but it still catches you every time (Sorge and van Witteloostuijn 2004, p. 1209).

From a scientific perspective, advocates of management fads present an easy target (for overviews, see Abrahamson 1996, p. 255; Jackson 2001, p. 17; Huczynski 2006, p. 6; Collins 2020, p. 52). The concepts are often so loaded with value formulations that it is easy to point out the internal contradictions in their practical implementation (for the classic account, see Pascale 1990, p. 18f). The empirical basis for management concepts is often no more than a simulation of scientific procedures, so poorly put together that in most cases it would not even stand up to methodological criticism from students in their first semester (see, for example, Guest 1994, p. 5ff).

Alongside an industry that brings management concepts onto the market in ever shorter cycles, a separate genre has developed in which the current management fashion is taken apart. It now seems to be fashionable not only to constantly propagate catchy new management concepts, but also to write them off on the grounds, "We've seen it all before." In academic circles, debunking management fashions seems to have become a kind of mass sport. Critics of fashion criticism are bored by the constant repetition of the same line of argument, namely that "there's nothing new under the sun" (see Collins 2001a, p. 27). It is possible almost to get the impression—in a further reflexive twist—that it is fashionable nowadays not only to criticize management fashions, but to criticize the repeated criticisms of management fashions.

We shouldn't overlook the fact that it can sometimes make sense to take advantage of the current management fashion to mount a critique based on organizational science. For teachers at universities and colleges of technology, it can be helpful to have students analyze current management fashions so that they understand the difference between academic-sounding self-descriptions in management literature and properly distanced external descriptions by organizational scientists (see Örtenblad et al. 2015). For an organizational researcher, it can be useful to work critically through a currently celebrated management fashion in order to bring old insights from organizational science to the notice of practitioners so that they can see the difference (for this approach, see Kühl 2020). In some cases, it may even make sense to initiate a small management fashion of one's own in order to fix scientifically sound considerations with respect to power, trust, and understanding in organizations in the minds of practitioners (for an attempt of this kind, see Kühl 2017).

Ultimately, however, from a detached practitioner's perspective, neither the ballyhoo surrounding the introduction of a new management concept nor the criticism that inevitably follows is any cause for satisfaction. On the one hand, a modicum of organizational experience is enough to stop you from going into raptures when a new prize pig labeled agility, excellence, or quality is being paraded around management village. On the other hand, seasoned practitioners are also aware that it is difficult to escape the fashion that happens to be in vogue at a particular time. From this perspective, it pays to understand the very simple nature of management fashions and be able to make use of them for your own purposes.

The aim of this book is to show how management fashions can be used in organizational change processes. Even if members of organizations are well advised not to commit themselves body and soul to any current organizational concept, they may still be able to use it to initiate change processes in their organizations. Because a management fashion can always be interpreted one way or another, it may well serve as a catalyst for pragmatic solutions to current problems.

This book is part of our ongoing Management Compact series, in which we present the essentials of working in organizations against the background of modern organizational theory for practitioners. In addition to this volume, we have also published books on "Shaping organizations," "Influencing organizational culture," "Leading projects," "Developing strategies," "Developing mission statements," "Exploring markets," "Managing leadership," "Managing compliance," "Facilitating workshops," and "Lateral leadership." Because we have based them on the same basic ideas, attentive readers will find related lines of thought and similar formulations in these books. We deliberately use these overlaps to emphasize the essential unity of the thinking that underlies them.

I do not believe in "simplifying" texts for managers and consultants by means of an assemblage of bullet points, executive summaries, and graphics. In many cases, readers are intellectually underchallenged by these aids, the assumption being that they are unable to grasp central ideas without textual and visual help. In this book—as in all the other books in the series—there is only one element I use to make reading the book easier, besides the single graphic illustrating the meta-structure matrix that appears in every book. I use small boxes to—on the one hand—cite empirical examples from organizations to illustrate a particular idea and—on the other—show how concrete management fashions can be analyzed with the support of organizational theory. If you are short of time, you can skip the contents of these boxes without losing the central theme of the book.

This book was developed as part of the Metaplan professional program "Leading and Consulting in Discourse." We would like to thank the participants from various year groups, who have not only critically questioned the approach presented here, but have also fed back their own practical experience. We would also like to express our gratitude to the organizational scientists who have critically reflected and commented on Metaplan's practice on many occasions during recent decades, particularly with regard to understanding management fashions.

Bielefeld, Germany   Stefan Kühl

Contents

About the Author

Stefan Kühl is Professor of Organizational Sociology at Bielefeld University and works as a consultant for Metaplan, particularly in dealing with ministries, administrations, companies, and associations.

1

What Is a Management Fashion?

In discussions about management concepts, it is often possible to achieve an effect simply by running through a list of the management fashions that have been propagated in recent decades: "organic organizational structure," "the synthetic organization," "adhocracy," "Theory Z," "Model J," "System 5," "integrative-innovative systems," the "multicellular organization," "lean enterprise," "reengineered enterprise," "the modular factory," "the fractal factory," the "responsive organization," "requisite organization," "learning organization," "intelligent organization," "the knowledge-creating company," "the collaborative enterprise," "the multicellular enterprise," "the centerless corporation," the "boundaryless organization," "horizontal organization," "self-managed organization," "dynamically robust organization," "agile organization," "adaptive organization," "resilient organization," "Teal organization," "holacratic organization," "conversational company," "collegially led organization," or "beta organization" (for examples of such lists, see Pascale 1990; DiMaggio 2001; Bort 2015).

The monotonous sequence alone provides initial access to management fashions. It illustrates how catchy names are generated so that management concepts strike a chord with recipients. It gives an impression of the speed with which they are brought onto the market and then replaced

© The Author(s), under exclusive license to Springer Nature Switzerland AG 2026
S. Kühl, *Making use of Management Fashions*,
https://doi.org/10.1007/978-3-032-09265-6_1

by others. It makes it possible to examine which fashions are still remembered and which have disappeared from the collective memory.

But what are management fashions?

1.1   Management Fashions: A Definition

Management fashions—or, in more general terms, management concepts—are widely shared ideas about how companies, administrations, hospitals, universities, schools, armies, police forces, or associations can be better organized. They are a system of assumptions, principles, and rules that enable managers to assess a situation, question their own practices, and consider alternative courses of action (Kramer 1975, p. 47).

Their knowledge content is arranged in such a way that the recommendations for action do not relate simply to a single organization, but are intended to be helpful to a large number of them. In some cases, a management concept is limited to one type of organization—for example, only to companies, administrative bodies, or armies. However, a concept will often jump from one type of organization to another, so that administrations and universities adopt concepts that were originally designed for companies, or companies adapt concepts that have proven successful in armies.

Management fashions promise to increase the adaptability, performance, and innovative capacity of organizations by introducing new design principles. Different concepts for the design of organizations are not placed side by side on an equal footing, instead the impression is conveyed that one of these concepts is superior to all the rest. This classification of concepts into those that are more and those that are less suitable addresses organizations' widespread need to eliminate perceived shortcomings and tap into previously unused opportunities for improvement (P. P. Carson et al. 2000, p. 1143 f.).

1.1.1 The "Invention" of Management Fashions

The people who significantly influence each other in the development of a management fashion may come from different backgrounds (in this connection see Huczynski 1993b, p. 40ff.). Some are anchored in science and present their reflections as findings from empirical research (see e.g. Porter 1980; Kanter 1983; Senge 1990; or Scharmer 2009b). Some develop their concepts from their consulting businesses and present them as the outcome of contacts with a variety of different organizations (see e.g. Peters and Waterman 1982; Laloux 2014). Others present their organizational concept as a quintessence of their work as top managers in top organizations (see e.g. Iacocca 2007; Hsieh 2010).

Some management fashions are immediately associated with one or two "inventors." This has led to the development of a small industry run by "management gurus" in which once popular researchers, consultants, and managers try to keep "their" management concept in the discussion (cf. Huczynski 1993b, p. 6; Huczynski 1993a, p. 446; D. Collins 2020, p. 6f.). As for other management fashions such as "organizational learning" and "agility," while it is possible to show how they became popular with management, no one has ultimately succeeded in ensuring that the concept is primarily associated with their name.

The success of management fads is based on the fact that a large number of presenters, consultants, and trainers jump on the bandwagon (cf. D. Collins 2000, p. 78ff.; D. Collins 2020, p. 45ff.). They propagate the ideas through their own books, articles, and blog posts, in which they rework the basic principles of the fashion in question. They present the concept at seminars and conferences, enriching it with their own reflections. They translate the often abstract notions into training concepts, which they underpin with their own experiences. Last but not least, they support organizations during implementation by offering suitable tools and methods for putting the management model into practice.

1.1.2   The Difference Between Management Fashions and Management Concepts

Management fashions—like fashions in general—don't last (Abrahamson 1996, p. 255). Often a management fashion is only the focus of general attention for a very short time and then it quickly loses its appeal. In many cases, management fashions wear out slowly, but sometimes they go out of favor very quickly because it soon becomes clear that the far-reaching promises they made are not going to be fulfilled (Miller et al. 2004, p. 7). A new "hot" management

---

The Sociology of Fashion

The central characteristic of fashions is their transience. All fashions are subject to a specific cycle of emergence, spread, and decline. This distinguishes them from social phenomena such as habitus, habits, style, or innovation. In the case of fashions in clothing, musical styles, and management concepts, their "inventors" dream that they have not simply produced a brief "flash in the pan," but have created a "classic" that will outlive them. However, this hope is often dashed—if not before, then when their idea is replaced by the next in line.

You can learn a lot about fashions in management by looking at the mechanisms that operate in other areas—in clothing, music, beard shapes, first names, or even methods of execution. Even if the proponents of management concepts resist the comparison by pointing to the irrationality of many other fashions, there are a number of similarities (see Clark and Greatbatch 2016, p. 402).

A key characteristic of fashions is that they work "contagiously." As with clothing, music styles, first names, or methods of execution, there are pioneers in organizational fashion, who are followed at some point by a great many others (see Aspers 2005). It is not possible to know in advance who the pack leader is going to be, but as soon as one emerges, more and more people follow them. A process of social contagion takes place that is increasingly difficult to escape from. Eventually the social pressure becomes so strong that non-participants have to justify why they are not "following the fashion."

The "penetrating power" of a fashion can become so intense at its peak that the burden of proof shifts fundamentally (Esposito 2004, p. 14). Whereas people still have to justify why they have an extravagant hairstyle, choose an unusual first name for their child, or question the hierarchical principle in an organization, when a fashion first emerges, once it catches on, the boot is on the other foot. Then people who don't let their hair grow long, don't choose one of the top 100 male or female first names when naming their children, or still put forward arguments in favor of hierarchy in organizations are the ones who have to justify themselves. Those who go with the fashion choose to be on the safe side—those who want to avoid it have to justify themselves.

On the one hand, a "trickle-down effect" can be observed in the implementation of fashions (on fashions as "class fashions," see Simmel 2012, p. 21ff.). It is argued that fashions are oriented towards the dominant class. In the case of fashions in dress, this may be the members of the upper class who are imitated by everybody else; in the case of executions, it may be the particularly efficient methods used in totalitarian states; in the case of management fashions, it is likely to be whatever is the rule in particularly successful large companies. Conversely, there is also a "trickle-up effect" in which the emergence of fashions can be traced back to "outsiders." Fashions in clothing may be based on styles adopted by people on the more disreputable fringes of society, execution methods on the practices of otherwise despised "pariah states," and management fashions on hip micro-organizations that have only existed for a few years (see also Simmel 2012, p. 25).

Fashions certainly play a role in modern society that should not be underestimated, because they provide orientation, at least for a certain period of time. But it would definitely be an exaggeration to describe them as a "central mechanism" in modern society (e.g. Blumer 1969, p. 290). Just as you cannot understand organizations by concentrating on an analysis of current management fashions, you cannot understand society by looking at what is fashionable at any particular time. You can, however, gain a small insight into the functioning of societies in general and organizations in particular by analyzing the laws that govern fashions.

concept coming onto the market displaces one that was previously top of the pops.

Whether a proposal is seen as a classic form of organization, a management concept, a tried and trusted formula, best practice or a management fad or even a short-lived trend depends on the perspective of the observer (for a differentiation between fashions and fads in the English-language literature, see e.g. Furnham 2004; on different designations see Sturdy et al. 2019). While critics of a particular proposal may point out that it merely resurrects a long-established organizational principle and predict that it will therefore soon disappear, its advocates would be devaluing their own concept if they were to present it merely as a management fashion. Supporters dream that they have found a new form of organization that will be regarded as classic in a few decades' time; sceptics point out that it is merely a rehash of well-known principles that will quickly turn out to be a dangerous management fad (cf. Miller and Hartwick 2002; Miller, Hartwick, and Le Breton-Miller 2004).

From a more distanced position, one might argue that it is only possible to judge whether a management concept is a transient fashion or a timeless principle after a certain lapse of time. If a management concept fades over time, this is a clear indication that it was a fashion. If it is still under discussion decades later and is being talked about in books on management, there is good reason to suppose that it enshrines principles that are largely timeless.

1.2 Management Fashions: A Classification in the Meta-Structure Matrix

In order to understand the impact of management methods, it is useful to work with the meta-structure matrix. In one dimension, it distinguishes three types of structure—communication channels, programs, and personnel (for details, see Luhmann 2000, p. 256ff.). In the other, it specifies three forms in which expectations are generated in organizations—on the show side, the formal side, and the informal side.

1.2.1 The Three Types of Structure in Organizations

Management fashions generally focus on one type of structure and define the requirements for the other two types from there. Some management methods choose communication channels as their starting point—i.e. the way in which communication can, and indeed has to, take place within the organization—and then define the program structure and the personnel requirements on that basis. Others take the programs—the target systems, service instructions, or IT programs—as the starting point and derive the communication channels and personnel structure from them. Others again take personnel as their starting point and consider what communication channels and what programs can be used to make them operate particularly effectively. If you take a closer look at the types of structure, you can gain an initial insight into the design of management methods.

Taking *communication channels* as the first type of structure: hierarchies, co-signing rights, and project structures determine which people should communicate with one another and which should not. When formal communication channels are defined, the possibilities for communication within the organization are initially severely restricted. Only a small number of legitimate communication channels are admitted, which members must use if they do not want to jeopardize their membership. Every organization therefore initially restricts a "basic condition of human possibilities," namely that "everyone can always communicate with everyone else about anything" (Luhmann 1970, p. 7). What you then have to try to do is to define the communication channels that are particularly suitable for an organization.

Many management fashions take communication channels as their starting point and complain about basic hierarchical structure and division into departments. Management concepts such as "organic corporate form" (Burns and Stalker 1961), the "synthetic organization" (Thompson 1967), the "adhocracy" (Toffler 1971), "System 5" (Likert and Araki 1986), the "integrative-innovative system"

(Kanter 1983) and the "multicellular organization" (Landier 1987), all aim to reduce hierarchical levels and make departmental boundaries more permeable. The concepts of the "collaborative enterprise" (Campbell and Goold 2000), the "horizontal organization" (Ostroff 1999), the "self-managed organization" (Purser and Cabana 1998), the "agile organization" (after Beck et al. 2001), the "Teal organization" (Laloux 2014) or the "talkative company" (Turco 2016) are ultimately nothing more than recyclings of concepts that focus on reducing hierarchies and dissolving departmental silos under new names.

Organizations use *programs*, the second basic type of structure, to determine the conditions under which decisions are accepted as correct. Orientation by means of its formal programs is made a condition of membership in the organization. Remaining in the organization becomes de facto impossible if you openly reject them. A first possibility for a formal "programming of an organization" arises when conditional programs in the form of written or computerized work processes are defined. These are if–then programs that lay down precisely how a member has to respond to a previously defined input such as a customer inquiry, a building application, or a situation in which someone runs amok in a school. A second possibility is when purpose programs come to be defined in the form of operational target systems, strategic objectives, or target agreements. At this point decisions are made regarding the objectives or goals that the organization is setting out to achieve. However, the choice of means to achieve them remains free within a given framework (for a distinction between program types, see Luhmann 1973, p. 101ff.; Luhmann 2000, p. 263ff.).

Management fashions can be differentiated according to whether they see more benefit in a conditional programming of the organization or whether they prefer to rely on purpose programming. Taylorism—certainly one of the most prominent and influential of management concepts—promises increases in efficiency and quality by consistently programming the organization with "if-then rules." The Taylorist concept of scientific management is based on the idea that work planning should decide systematically what work processes ought to look like, and the workers should then be obliged to follow these optimized procedures slavishly (see Taylor 1967). Conditional programming has certainly lost its popularity as a basis for management concepts—not least due to criticism of Taylorism. Ultimately, however, concepts such as total quality management (Ishikawa 1987), lean management (Womack, Jones, and Roos 1990), and business process reengineering (Hammer and Champy 1993) are based on conditional programming of the organization, except that employees are given more opportunities to have a say. However, management concepts that rely on purpose programming are more in vogue nowadays because employees are given the freedom to determine the means for achieving the purposes themselves. "Management by objectives" (Drucker 1954; Odiorne 1965) and "leadership in the employee relationship" (Höhn 1966) were the first detailed concepts for goal-oriented management programs. "Management by agreements on targets" and "objectives and key results" were ultimately only attempts to revive the principle of management-by-objectives programs (see especially Grove 1983).

Personnel, the third central structural element in organizations, denotes the attempt to influence which decisions are made in an organization through decisions regarding staff. There are various formal ways for organizations to make personnel decisions—through hiring, firing, internal transfers, and personnel development (cf. Luhmann 1971, p. 208). Formal requirement profiles are defined for positions, economic or legal criteria for dismissals are worked out, official career paths are defined or mandatory personnel development measures are developed for all employees. In this way, an organization initially limits its ability to recruit and move personnel, but in doing so creates the basis for integrating thousands or tens of thousands of employees into an organization in the first place.

Many management concepts take personnel considerations as their starting point. The "human relations approach," which developed 90 years ago in contrast to Taylorist forms of work, presented itself as a concept that focuses on people (see the classic works by Mayo 1933 and Roethlisberger and Dickson 1939, though these are now rarely read in their entirety). Under concepts such as "humanocracy," this idea is now being revisited and the view propagated that an organization can only function if the potential of its employees is awakened (see, for example, Hamel and Zanini 2020). According to the these people-centered management fashions, organizations can only be innovative, efficient, and effective if employees are able develop freely and thus derive a high level of satisfaction from their work (for criticism of this "cow sociology"—contented cows give more milk—see Huczynski 2006, p. 45).

1.2.2   The Three Sides of Organizations

In order to understand more precisely how management fashions work in organizations and what functions they fulfil, it makes sense to distinguish between three sides in an organization (for a more detailed account, see Kühl 2021, p. 88ff.). Advocates of management concepts claim that new organizational principles should not only be on display on the organization's show side, but should also be anchored in its formal structures and thus also produce informal effects. When management fashions are adopted, however, there is often only a loose connection between what is presented on the show side and the way in which the concept is implemented in the communication channels, the programs, and the criteria applicable to staff as well as the effect it has on the organizational culture and informal expectations. However, this does not necessarily have to be problematic; it may give the organization the flexibility it requires in the design of its organizational structures.

An organization's "show side" is its facade. It needs to make a statement of some kind through its decorations, ornamentation, or even just through its regularity. Organizations present as attractive a "façade" as possible to the outside world in order to gain the favor of customers, generate a positive attitude in the mass media, or ensure their legitimation by political forces is maintained. What goes on at the back of the "store" is not completely unimportant, but in many cases the survival of an organization depends largely on the "façade" with its "shop windows" being suitably spruced up. Consequently, the successful management of organizations always includes aspects of the "performing arts" (Mangham 1990, p. 105).

The implementation of management fashions always has a direct impact on the show side of an organization. Its reputation will be enhanced if its management declares that the importance of the hierarchy will be reduced and its employees will largely be able to organize themselves in future. Its prestige will increase if it lets it be known that, within the framework of a jointly negotiated set of objectives, its employees can decide for themselves how they want to achieve their goals. It can contribute to the reputation of an organization if the management emphasizes that its future success will depend on the qualifications of its employees and that everything is therefore being done to attract and retain top performers. The effect of adapting to management fashions on the show side should not be underestimated, because success depends not only on rapid adaptation to environmental changes, innovative product development, and efficient processes, but also on the legitimacy that an organization has within its environment (for this idea, see Meyer and Rowan 1977, p. 352ff.).

The *formal side is* the official set of rules by which members feel themselves to be bound. The central feature of organizations is that they can make membership conditional: The condition is that you have to make a decision whether you are willing to accept the organization's expectation structures. It specifies how long you have to be present on the organization's premises, what time you start, what time you finish, what you have to do while you are there, which other members of the organization you have to pay heed to, and which you can ignore. If you are not prepared to adhere to these expectations, you cannot remain a member of the organization. The formal structures are, to use a somewhat unwieldy phrase, the "predetermined principles governing decision making" in an organization to which its members must adhere.

The claim of the proponents of management concepts is that the principles they propagate have a direct effect on the formal structure of the organization. In many cases, however, environmental requirements can be satisfied by symbolic measures carried out on the show side of the organization. The communications department sets up a new mission statement, the personnel development department purchases new training courses, and the quality assurance department adjusts its observation grids. Of course, in many cases such measures do not leave the organization unaffected, but only very rarely are there immediate effects in the form of fundamentally changed formal expectations.

The show side of the organization, which is responsible for maintaining its legitimacy, and the formal side remain

The Case of an Organizational Model with a Direct Effect on the Formal Structure

There are some management methods that are more successful than others in having a direct impact on the formal structure (for details, see Kühl 2023). The holacratic organizational concept, which was popular in management discourse for a while, uses a clever trick to achieve the dissolution of departmental boundaries and the softening of hierarchies: a detailed formal fixing of every conceivable expectation to which members of the organization are subject. Every assignment of a task, every allocation to a group, every shift in responsibilities, no matter how small, is recorded in the organization's control software for all to see. This results in a large number of detailed descriptions of the roles carried out by all the members of the organization, which can be compiled into comprehensive, individualized job descriptions. This fixation down to the smallest detail of the expectations laid upon organization members can be described as hyperformalization.

The formal order of holacratic organizations is protected by the fact that they commit to holacratic principles by signing up to a "constitution" almost 50 pages long, that regulates every detail of the organization's governance (see Robertson 2015, 23). The interlocking of the elements specified in the constitution is secured by holacratic control software, which is used to map all formal communication and decision-making processes within an organization. Although organizations can decide not to use these software packages, the complexity becomes so great in an organization with upwards of 20 or 30 employees that it is extremely difficult to control holacratic organizations without this technical support.

The principles established by the holacratic constitution are so strongly fixed that any change is immediately enshrined as a formal expectation. This process is intensified by the fact that the management software leaves little room for deviation in the formal structure. Holacratic organizations—unlike many other organizations that adapt to management fashions—do not primarily change their external image, but rather their formal structure. Whether this is an advantage or a disadvantage remains to be seen.

largely uncoupled from the rest and changes there only seep into the organization in small doses.

We can speak of the *informal side of* an organization, that is its organizational culture, when an action that is not catered for in the formal structure occurs with a certain regularity. The "informal," the "sublife," the "culture" are the "undecided decision-making premises" that prevail in an organization (Rodríguez 1991, p. 140f.). The basic idea is simple: there are rules governing the way in which decisions are to be made in future within an organization that are arrived at not through decisions made by a company board, a party conference, or a pope, but which have simply crept in and successfully established themselves as habits.

The claim of management fashions is that they have a direct effect on the informal structures—the organizational culture—of a company, an administration, a hospital, or a school. The hope is that a management concept can shape the informal networks, hidden incentive structures, and implicit thought patterns so that they work in the interests of the organization. Altering the formal structure is supposed not only to change the "hard factors", but also to get the "soft factors" in the organizational culture under control. The challenge, however, lies in the fact that the informal structures—the organizational culture—are beyond the direct control of management.

The extent to which management fashions radiate from the public face to the formal side and thus also to the informal side varies not only from concept to concept, but also from organization to organization. Some management concepts are worked out in such detail that it is difficult to use them simply for presentation purposes on the show side. Commitment to a management concept therefore almost inevitably leads to changes in the formal structure of the organization, even if any deviations are often only informal ones. Other management concepts are so abstract that many organizations use them primarily to give themselves a modern façade. Even so, some do use them to make deep interventions in the formal structure. Precisely because these management concepts leave a lot of room for interpretation, interventions made in the name of a currently fashionable model often vary greatly from organization to organization.

2

Beyond the Rational Idea of Management Fashions

Making use of management fashions involves luring the designers of organizational processes with visions of a better future. It entails painting a "beautiful picture" of what could be achieved with the organization through a change process. Management gurus rough out the outline of a lean enterprise, an agile organization, or a knowledge-based system and consulting firm and, for an appropriate fee, provide the color elements so that each organization can then paint its own picture of an enticing future based on the templates (for how the players interact, see Barley and Kunda 2004).

Ultimately, all management fashions are based on an "aestheticization" of organizational futures (see Neuberger 1994). In this process, an image of a possible better organization, which contrasts positively with the reality experienced in everyday life, is drawn with the aid of comprehensive concept papers, original organizational charts, and colorful network plans. The images of a possible organization created by management fashions pander to managers' yearning for coherent, harmonious, and comprehensive works of art, but without exposing them to recriminations on account of the discrepancy between their own reality and this image. On the contrary: the discrepancy between the real dynamics, diversity, and ambiguity of the

© The Author(s), under exclusive license to Springer Nature Switzerland AG 2026
S. Kühl, *Making use of Management Fashions*,
https://doi.org/10.1007/978-3-032-09265-6_2

organization and the harmonious and coherent overall picture provided serves to justify the change processes driven by management.

How are these management models built in detail? What is their appeal for organizational designers? And where are the blind spots in this view of organizations?

2.1   The Promises of Management Fashions

Management concepts are based on a form of construction that is known to science as the purpose-driven organizational model. The starting point is always a "primary purpose"—the production of dishwashers, the construction of hotel buildings, the sale of legal (or illegal) drugs, or the enforcement of stricter limit values for particulate matter. Irrespective of what the "original purpose" of the organization may have been, the justification for its existence lies solely in its fulfilment of that purpose. The promoters of management concepts promise to have the appropriate levers at their disposal to specify, modify, operationalize, and adapt these "original purposes." Despite all the variations in detail, management concepts are all based on the same design.

2.1.1   The Dramatization of Social Challenges

Dramatic social changes are used to justify a new management style. The world is becoming ever more complex, developments are increasingly difficult to predict, and forecasts are based on ever more uncertain assumptions. There is talk of an increasing scarcity of raw materials, a growing risk of terrorist attacks and regional wars, an increase in the number of natural disasters, the threat of ecological collapse, an increase in national debt, a shortage of time as a resource, and growing social inequality, all of which pose completely new challenges for organizations (see, for example, Kotter 2014, p. 3ff.).

Everyone acknowledges that the old organizational model of "predicting and controlling" worked well in the classic industrial age. In the past, organizations were able to achieve both "lasting stability" and "growing success" through "forward planning, central control, and the avoidance of deviations from strategy." The idea would have been based on developing "the 'perfect' system in advance" to avoid trouble in future. But in the post-industrial world, according to the usual argument put forward by the proponents of management fashions, we now face fundamentally "new challenges" such as "growing complexity, increasing transparency, greater interconnectedness at all levels, shorter time horizons, economic and ecological instability" (as exemplified by Robertson 2015, p. 12f.). When the promoters of management fashions offer a diagnosis of the state of the times, their diagnoses invariably emphasize that there have never been such fundamental social changes taking place as there are now. Regardless of whether you take a management fashion from the early 1920s, the period after the Second World War, the 1970s—characterized by the oil shock, the 1990s—defined by the end of the Cold War, the period before the turn of the century—dominated by a strong influx of venture capital or the 2010s—it will never fail to stress that at no time has there ever been a period in which the technical revolutions, economic challenges, and social upheaval have been as fundamental as they are now. Even if it is conceded that there have been fundamental changes before, it is always suggested that we are now living in particularly turbulent times that urgently require a response from organizations. A certain alarmism seems to be an inevitable part of the presentation of management fashions.

2.1.2 The Need for Revolutionary Change

Classic organizational models, according to the usual dramatized accompaniment to the propagation of new management concepts, do not have "the agility that is necessary in this environment of rapid change and complexity" and are unable to spark the "enthusiasm and creativity of employees" required for the challenge. "Today's organizations," by general consent, are "outdated" (as exemplified by Robertson 2015, p. 12f.). Those who cling to outdated organizational principles—in the monotonously repeated phraseology of the promoters of management fashions—risk the "being punished with extinction."

Nothing less than a revolutionary change in the way organizations structure themselves is called for. Management gurus, organizational consultants, and even some organizational scientists do not hesitate to speak of the "need for a revolution" (Peters 1988, p. 3ff.) a "real revolution" (Crozier 1989, p. 21) or even a "cultural revolution" (Landier 1991). "Stage directions for revolutionaries" (Tichy 1995) "manifestos for business revolutions" (Hammer and Champy 1993) and "manuals for a management revolution" (Peters 1988) have appeared addressed to management. Management fads are presented as "revolutionary management system[s] for a volatile world" (Robertson 2015). In view of the demand in management discourse for a "permanent revolution", observers have noted that Leon Trotsky or Mao Zedong would have turned "green with envy" (Micklethwait and Wooldrige 1996, p. 14).

Because the word "revolution" also threatened to wear thin in management discourse at some point, it was replaced by the word "disruption" in many organizations. Disruptions are innovations that replace existing products, services, or technologies within a short period of time (Christensen 1998). For fear of missing out on such disruptive trends, organizations now appoint "Chief Disruption Officers," business media regularly proclaim the "Disrupter of the Year," congresses now refer to themselves as "Disruption Potential," and an ordinary consulting company treats itself to the byname "The Disruption Consultancy."

Both the term "revolution" and the term "disruption" combine the fear of not being able to cope with the supposedly dramatic challenges with a solution—namely to become a revolutionary pioneer oneself. The old idea of the economist Joseph Schumpeter (1947), the need for "creative destruction" as the basis for progress, is reformulated here as a requirement for organizations.

2.1.3   The Promise of a Solution to Classic Organizational Problems

Problems inevitably arise in organizations owing to the division of labor. If the members no longer fit around a kitchen table, the work has to be divided up. This creates subunits within the organization that concentrate on individual tasks. They inevitably develop their own local rationalities, so that the perspective of the concerns and needs of other units goes increasingly out of focus. Coordination problems and power struggles are the inevitable result.

The inventors and promoters of management fads promise that they have found a way to prevent exactly that. They raise the hope that they have developed a model with which organizations can free themselves from "trench warfare, bureaucracy and competition," from "stress," "burnout," and "resignation" and "from pompous behavior at the top and exhausting work at the lower levels." They promise to have developed a model that "makes work productive, fulfilling and meaningful," that "creates soulful workplaces" in which talents "can flourish" and "vocations are valued" (see, for example, Laloux 2015, p. 11).

What we have here is an idealization of the future and at the same time a "maligning" of the past. Change projects, change processes, and reforms here take the form of descriptions of deficiencies based on the assumption that things can be done better. The past is portrayed negatively so that the future will look better. Factual reality is pumped up with counterfactual ideals in order to nurture the hope that the organization will eventually improve in the direction of these ideals and that all employees will be convinced of what is "good, important, and right."

This discrepancy between the "actual state" and the "target state" is used as a key driver in many change processes. Energy is generated by the fact that the master plans, visions, and target states appear more attractive, simpler, and more plausible than the perceived reality, which is problematic, complex, and chaotic. It is suggested that the consulting process enables organizations to achieve a more coherent, consistent, and ultimately more rational way of functioning, from which all employees can ultimately benefit. The good intentions of the change projects are difficult to refute because the "acid test of their plans" is still pending (Luhmann 2000, p. 338).

2.1.4 The Progress Model in Management Fashions

On the way to revolutionary management systems, most management fashions work with more or less simple progress models. In these, organizations develop away from the model of the pack (characterized by an all-determining boss), through the model of the army (characterized by regularity), or a model of the organization primarily oriented towards efficiency, to a concept of the family (characterized by a combination of a classic hierarchy and a high degree of independence), until they finally become the epitome of a network consisting of self-organizing units (for what follows. See Laloux 2015, p. 36f.).

Such models of organizational forms that are constantly evolving for the better can be easily combined with the development of leadership roles. According to the story, the idea of the big boss with a strict hierarchy is followed by the idea of combining classic top-down leadership with shared leadership. After the development of shared organizational leadership comes the principle of democratic leadership, according to which employees choose their own bosses, ending in a leaderless organization characterized by the absolute equality of all members.

Sometimes the development stages are also highlighted with colors to make it even easier to locate them. A magenta-colored organization characterized by an impulsive leadership style would be followed by an amber-yellow system dominated by formal leadership, which would be replaced by an orange structure characterized by performance. This would then be followed by a green organization characterized by participation, which in the final stage would lead to a shimmering blue-green company characterized by completely new forms of cooperation (Laloux 2014 provides a particularly colourful presentation).

Consultants operationalize such suggestions of progress in management concepts in maturity models (for an early disquisition on leadership, see Hersey and Blanchard 1969). Under labels such as "People Capability Maturity Model," "Organizational Project Management Maturity Model," or "Quality Management Maturity Grid," instruments are developed that give the impression that organizations can be "objectively" assessed according to the "maturity level" they have achieved in one dimension (for an overview, see Wendler 2012). On the basis of comprehensive assessments, road maps can then be drawn up to help organizations reach the next level. Organizations are given the impression that they have a deficit, but at the same time are shown how they can reduce this deficit. Even if the classification into maturity levels is highly contrived, the comparison with supposedly "more mature" organizations on its own creates a pressure to act.

The more or less explicit suggestions of progress have an important function for management fashions. Every management fashion threatens to signal failure on the part of a management. After all, they have not yet introduced the principle propagated in the management fashion and have thus exposed their organization to risk. By presenting the principle as the next step in a progress model, however, managers are reassured; adopting the management fashion is merely a matter of taking the next step in the organization's development toward something (even) better.

2.1.5 Highlighting the Benefits: For the Individual and for Society

Social processes are usually characterized by the fact that what benefits one group harms another. If salaries are cut, this is at the expense of the employees, but it benefits the employers because of the cost savings. If car companies successfully push through higher limits for nitrogen oxides, this is beneficial for them because they save on the costs of exhaust gas purification—but for city dwellers, this brings health disadvantages in the form of an increased incidence of asthma, strokes, or heart attacks. Many advantages can only be achieved by externalizing the disadvantages, i.e. passing them on to others. In game theory, this is known as a zero-sum game. The gain of one person can only be achieved through the loss of another.

Contrary to the view that the benefit of some means harm to others, management fads promise that, with their support, these zero-sum games can be stopped short. If their central principle is implemented in organizations, everyone will ultimately benefit, so the promise goes. Employees will be happier, organizations will be more efficient, and customers will be more satisfied thanks to better product quality. Communities will benefit from more innovative organizations, the environment will be less polluted, and the world as a whole will become a better place. In game theory, this is called a win-win situation. A gain for some is also a gain for others.

In management fashions, this idea of a win-win situation is particularly evident in the fact that the promise of happiness applies not only at the meso level of the organization, but also at the micro level of each individual. According to the promise, the concept is no longer just about increasing effectiveness, efficiency, and innovation in the organization, but also about enabling growth potential for the individual.

Moreover, society as a whole will benefit fundamentally from the management model in question, according to the repeated promise. Companies with a classic organizational form are, according to the usual way a management fashion is presented, characterized by an "unhealthy autonomy" and ignore their "responsibility towards the wider world." The management concept, however, will have the potential "without any chaotic revolutions" to transcend our classic notion of national governments by means of a new kind of "globally integrative power structure." A "new kind of integrated nervous system and decision-making nexus for the world" will emerge (for a typical account, see Robertson 2016, 4,16,19). The end result will be—this is, more or less explicitly, the promise of every management concept—a

---

"Healing" the World

A Typical Management Fashion Rescue Fantasy

The learning organization was long regarded as the most popular way to implement change projects in organizations, until organizational developers and systemic consultants began to propagate Otto Scharmer's Theory U. Theory U was a phase model designed to achieve a state desired by everyone involved. According to Scharmer, the first phase, the "downloading" phase, starts at the upper left-hand end of an imaginary "U". This is followed—down the left-hand side of the "U"—by the phase of "looking," in which the "judgments brought along" should be let go and a fresh look should be taken at "reality." According to Scharmer, this phase is about "opening up thinking." This is followed by the phase of "sensing," in which everyone has to "connect with the field, immerse themselves and look at the situation as a whole" and thus achieve an "opening of feeling." This is followed by a phase where the aim is to "open the will," and "letting go" and "letting come" phases, in which one connects with the "inner source." Having figuratively arrived at the bottom of the "U", all participants should now ask themselves who they are and what their own task is in the "inner place of stillness" through a process known as "presencing." As a result of a renewed "opening of feeling," the visions that have emerged from this "deeper source" should then be crystallized in a phase of "condensing". Then, through a renewed "opening of thinking", the "future should be explored and developed together through practical action". In the final phase of "performing" the "new" is to be brought "into form" through a change in everyday practices (Scharmer 2009a, 62 f.).

The starting point for a management fashion is the diagnosis of a dramatic crisis—this is also the case with Theory U. According to Scharmer, the current crisis is not simply that of the individual manager or the individual organization or a particular country—it is a crisis of society as a whole. "While the pressure around us is increasing and the degrees of freedom are decreasing," the unintended side effects and consequences of our actions are multiplying. Despite a "flourishing global economy," "three billion people are living in poverty." We spend "vast sums of money on healthcare systems" that "poke around at the symptom level and are unable to address the root causes of health and disease in our society." We "dump large amounts of money into our education systems, but have been unable to create schools and institutions of higher learning that mobilize the deep human capacity to learn" (Scharmer 2007, p. 203). If this dramatic exaggeration is to be believed, we live on "a thin crust of order and stability that can break apart at any time" (Scharmer 2009a, p. 22).

In response to this crisis, Scharmer proclaims, we need "major transformations." According to him, what matters now are completely "new actions," creating "new structures," "setting up new processes," establishing a "new way of thinking," and creating a "new self" as part of a process of "re-acting," "re-structuring," "re-designing," "re-framing," and "re-generating". It is not enough just to change organizations or individual aspects of the organization. The aim is to change people's "selves" and thereby raise "society" as a whole to a new level of development. This is a line of argument that is typical of management fashions. The starting point is changes that need to take place in organizations, but the claim is that changes made to organizations will change society as a whole for the better. We are talking about the "micro, meso, macro, and mundo levels of social systems," which can be reached and changed by Theory U (Scharmer 2009a, p. 235).

But it is precisely at this point that Theory U—like almost all other management methods—falls short. Social systems function very differently at different levels (vgl. Grundlegend Luhmann 1975). Face-to-face interaction, which is based on communication between those present, functions very differently from a market in which goods and services are traded with a time delay and over a large spatial distance. A family with its focus on intimate communication has a completely different logic than an organization with its focus on communicating decisions or a protest movement with its focus on communicating values. And changes in the communication within a team are based on fundamentally different principles from changes in society.

This process, which is referred to as "social differentiation" in sociological systems theory, is negated by Theory U. It is clear from the case descriptions of people who work with Theory U, that its primary use is to clarify the positions of individuals in teams or groups. When Otto Scharmer tries to describe how Theory U can be used to achieve organizational or even social change, these processes remain surprisingly watery and indistinct. It all boils down to such hapless ideas as that society can be changed by people all over the world listening to his online courses on Theory U and then meeting in real or virtual circles to change society. The idea that such far-reaching efforts to bring about change can be produced by short-term communal experiences at more or less virtual gatherings is an illusion. It has nothing to do with a fundamental understanding of the differentiation in modern societies.

better world—with greater prosperity, less pollution, and fewer conflicts.

2.2 The Charm of Management Fashions

The appeal of management fashions for practitioners is enhanced by the fact that the purpose-driven organizational model presented is enriched with a number of attractive "ingredients." The focus is on an organizational principle that management can use as a guide. Methods are presented for implementing the concept in practice. The reference to pioneering organizations serves as proof that other organizations have massively increased their innovative strength, efficiency, and employee satisfaction thanks to the management concept. The homeopathically interspersed references to theories serve to present the management concept as anchored in science.

2.2.1 Presenting a Recipe for Success

The number of possibilities available to organizations to adapt their structure in order to acquire a particular shape is finite. They can decentralize decisions in order to find locally adapted solutions or centralize them in order to streamline the organization. Organizations can flatten hierarchies and accept larger management spans or work with steep hierarchies to ensure that managers are approachable. An attempt can be made to bind staff to the organization long-term in order to benefit from their experience and loyalty, or to focus on a high degree of staff interchangeability in order to achieve greater flexibility. Employees can be managed by means of precise if–then rules, to achieve a high degree of work routinization, or by targets, where the choice of means is left to the employees within a certain framework. Overall, there are no more than a few dozen adjusting screws in organizations that can be turned in one direction or another.

In a management model, only one of these well-known principles is prominently singled out and all the other design principles are derived from it (see Kieser 1996, p. 23). Think of the division of the work process into the smallest possible packages as a basic principle of Taylorism (Taylor 1967), the propagation of internal entrepreneurship through the concept of intrapreneurship (Pinchot 1988), the consistent reduction of buffers in lean management (Womack, Jones, and Roos 1990), the propagation of a large-scale abandonment of formality in organizational culture (Peters and Waterman 1982), the focus on processes in the concept of business process reengineering (Hammer and Champy 1993), or the focus on the role and not the person in holacracy (Robertson 2015).

In all these cases an adjustment screw that has proven effective in dealing with a specific problem in individual organizational units is put forward as a guiding principle for the entire organization. The idea of dispensing with a supervisor in team working and making do with electing a spokesperson is jazzed up as a principle for the entire organization in the concept of the democratic enterprise. The basic idea behind agile programming methods, in which goals for software development are agreed from week to week instead of in a planning process intended to cover months or years, is then presented as the guiding principle for the entire organization in the agile organization model. The idea of formally defining the roles of members of the organization down to the smallest detail is successfully tested on assembly lines, in call centers, and in delivery services, and then elevated to a basic principle for the entire organization in hyperformalized management concepts.

2.2.2 The Development of Suitable Methods for a Management Model

Management concepts are enriched with a variety of management methods. Lean management is underpinned by methods such as Six Sigma, Kaizen, the Ishikawa diagram, the Shainin method of formulating problems, value stream mapping, the Plan Do Check Act method, or presentation on flow boards. The concept of the agile organization is underpinned by methods such as user stories, story mapping, prototyping, minimum viable product, customer journey, timeboxing, sprints, Kanban, backlog, daily stand-up, and retrospectives.

The function of methods is to convey the impression that a management concept can be implemented. Management fashions emphasize an organizational principle and otherwise often insist on vague value formulations that would leave the practitioner at a loss without additional support. The promise of more agility, greater resilience, greater responsiveness, radical streamlining, or increased process orientation sounds good, but leaves open how these can be implemented. By contrast, management methods are more tangible. They can be trained for in just a few days and applied in workshops.

Nowadays there are far too many management methods to count: design thinking, project structure planning, network planning technique, moderation method, stakeholder analysis, milestone trend, retrospective, scrum method, Six Sigma, Kanban, "program evaluation & review technique," "portfolio management," "stakeholder management," "intrapreneurship," "managerial grid," "benchmarking," "360-degree feedback," "one-minute management." "brainstorming," "moderation method," "management-by-walking-around," "zero base budgeting," "just-in-time,"

"Toolism" as an Expression of Helplessness

How Agile Working Methods Are Introduced in Ministries

There are good reasons to grant ministers a high degree of autonomy with respect to their departments. Their employees have the necessary specialist expertise in a subject to be able to implement laws or set up funding projects. Responsibility can be assigned to the ministers in question because they are not channelling an impulse from a presidential or prime ministerial office, but are driven forward by the ministries themselves.

The effect is a high degree of autonomy in shaping not only the policy of the individual department, but also its organization. Each ministry can use its central departments to define how its files should look, how draft legislation should be worked on, how staff appointments should be documented, how staff appraisals should be carried out, and how invoices should be paid. Each ministry has its own positions and budgets through which these procedures can be adapted to its specific requirements.

However, the increasing scope for digitization is highlighting more and more the disadvantages of ministerial autonomy in the design of their administrative processes. Electronic files are not compatible between ministries and have to be laboriously converted. Cross-departmental collaboration on draft legislation is made more difficult because each ministry uses its own procedures for working on a document. The transfer of personnel is made more difficult too because personnel files cannot be exchanged digitally between ministries.

Coordination committees are therefore being set up to strive for standardization between ministries at the level of state secretaries, heads of central departments, and unit heads. However, the effects are limited because the central departments of the individual ministries do not want to give up their autonomy in designing their own procedures or having a budget of their own at their disposal. Agreements are therefore reached in coordination committees that get regularly bogged down in terms of their concrete feasibility. In fact, no one dares to take on departmental sovereignty in administrative procedures because there are no political prizes to be won in public from doing so, but at the same

time there is a good chance of coming to grief owing to resistance from the individual ministries.

This leads to frustration, not least for employees who are
supposed to implement more agile forms of working in their
individual ministries. Although cross-departmental meet-
ings are held with colleagues from other ministries, they do
not get around to the relevant topics—establishing common
cross-departmental technical standards, the use of shared
servers by the ministries, or softening the division of ministries into sections that has been established for decades.

The employees are focused on promoting the use of agile
tools in the ministries. Workshops on design thinking are
held, individual departments are supported in their work
through retrospectives, Canvas (the virtual learning environment) is being introduced as a tool in departments, and
project groups are being trained in the implementation of
sprints. The hope is that these bottom-up measures will suc-
ceed in changing the way ministries work. In reality, however, these are merely symbolic actions that enable ministries to give themselves an agile image without
fundamentally changing the way they work. Agile "tool-
ism" thus conceals the inability to remove the structural
blockages in ministerial administration.

"quality circles" (for a list, see Glaser 1997). A separate
genre has developed of books that are concerned solely with
sorting these methods and presenting them in ever
new forms.

Management fashions draw on familiar management
methods and only occasionally develop new ones. Their
promoters make use of the familiar toolbox and merely
adapt the tools for their particular purposes. Familiar tools
are equipped with some new features so that while they
benefit from recognition value at the same time they do not
trigger the feeling that this is merely more of the same.

2.2.3   Praise for Pioneering Organizations

Simply proclaiming that a particular principle leads to success and presenting an array of management concepts is not enough. What is needed is the assurance that the principles in question do work. It is therefore crucial for the establishment of a management fashion that it should be exemplified in organizations that have become successful through the principle in question (for an early list, see Whyte 1951, p. 308 f.). It must appear as if "real managers" have used it to solve "real problems" in "real organizations" (Clark and Greatbatch 2016, p. 413). Presenting pioneering organizations that can be used to illustrate the application of management principles plays a central role in management fashions (Miller, Hartwick, and Le Breton-Miller 2004, p. 14).

There are two different variants: In one, organizations that are considered progressive are singled out and the inventor's own recipes for success are presented as the result of an analysis of these organizations (see for example Peters and Waterman 1982; J. Collins 2001; Laloux 2014). In the other variant, a collection of recipes for success is presented and then illustrated by reference to organizations that have achieved success by using them (see for example Womack, Jones, and Roos 1990; Hammer and Champy 1993; Robertson 2015).

It is often not possible to find out on what basis pioneering organizations are presented as such. We do not know how many interviews were conducted in the organization, what participant observations were carried out, and how the organization's documents were evaluated. Instead, the dominant feature is usually a more or less well-crafted piece of "storytelling." The pioneering organizations are described in the most illustrative language possible, the story centers

The Simplest Method for Producing a Pioneering Organization: Use Your Own Organization as a Role Model

The easiest way to identify a trailblazing organization is for consultants to present their own company as being one (for this phenomenon, see Kühl 2020, 174ff.). In this case, the consulting firm itself not only illustrates how the method is to be applied, its successes can be put down to its having applied the method. In the case of business process engineering, consulting firms praise a method by claiming that they have tripled their own efficiency by applying it. In the case of lean management, consulting firms claim that streamlining their own company has led to a significant reduction in costs.

In the lists of pioneering organizations, the high proportion of small consulting firms with a handful of employees, which often represent the introduction of a currently popular organizational model as their only product, is striking. In the books on management in which a particular management concept is touted as a model for the twenty-first century, consultancy micro organizations appear to function as the model for the organization of the future, despite claims that only the experience of larger organizations has been taken into account (see a particularly striking example in Laloux 2014, pp. 122, 129, 182, 217, 257f., 267 und 304).

But this reference by consultants to their own positive experiences with the application of a method that they themselves are selling is not sufficient proof of the worth of a management fashion in most cases. For this reason, the advocates of management concepts make a point of identifying organizations beyond their own consulting firm that have successfully implemented the concept they are propagating and are suitable for presentation as pioneers.

on a struggle with dramatic crises, and there is always an impressively happy ending.

Central to "storytelling" is that the story of success in an organization should be personalized (with respect to the examples below, see Kieser 1997b, p. 58). It is all about the discovery of lean management at the car manufacturer

Toyota, by Eiji Toyoda (later the CEO) and his "production genius" Taiichi Ohno (Womack, Jones, and Roos 1990, p. 51), about Percy Barnevik's vision of a consistently decentralized form of organization, developed by the CEO of the automation and energy company ABB (Peters 1992, p. 45), or about Tony Hsieh, who is said to have taken his company Zappos in a completely new direction through his hyperformalization (Robertson 2015, p. 18f.).

In the stories about the pioneering organizations, a simple causal relationship is established between the supposed success of the organization and a management principle. Increases in efficiency, innovative strength, or employee satisfaction are explained in a highly simplified manner by the application of a management principle. The fact that completely different factors—a general economic upturn, changes in management, or even just a lucky coincidence—could have contributed to the success of the organization is ignored (see Huczynski 2006, p. 232).

The stories about pioneering organizations then spread via simple copy and paste. In a management bestseller, an organization that the authors have got to know at best through a brief visit and a few conversations is praised as an example of a management principle that is being propagated. Then a process of largely untested adoption begins following the example of this pioneering organization. Consultants jump on the bandwagon and present the organization discussed in a management bestseller as a role model, often without having learned anything about it themselves from their own analysis. Managers who try to use a management fashion in their own organization present the organization discussed in the management bestseller as a role model, even though they have only got to know its show side and through a one-day company tour at most.

In the process of retelling the story, the image of the organization as a pioneer of the management principle in question is consolidated. If a story is told often enough, everyone will assume that it cannot be wrong. The result is that literature about these pioneering organizations haunts management discussions for years—sometimes even decades—even though it often has little to do with the organization that was originally praised in the management bestseller.

Behind the Scenes at an Organization that Pioneered Self-Organized Teams

Hardly any other topic has been dealt with as intensively and comprehensively in management literature as that of self-organized teams. The functioning of self-organized teams has now been described not only for the key automotive, mechanical engineering, electronics, and chemical industries, but also for companies in software development and the service sector, for organizations in public administration, for service providers in the care sector, and for hospitals. The management literature is full of success stories of companies that have introduced self-organized teams.

A well-known medium-sized supplier to the automotive industry—let's call it Ladra here—is introducing self-organizing teams under the label of semi-autonomous group work (for details, see Kühl 2015, p. 153ff.). The self-description of the management involved in the introduction, as well as the reports of the accompanying researchers, read like economic success stories. Ladra describes the effects of group work using keywords such as "higher profitability, lower overheads," "significant savings in overheads," "significant quality improvement and cost savings," and "improvement in international competitiveness through more cost-effective organization." It was noted that turnover per working hour has increased by 50 percent in six years. As a result, this company is celebrated in management literature as a model organization for self-organized teamwork.

The high level of attention the company received in management literature meant significantly improved career opportunities for its management. Ladra's HR manager moved to another company as one of the pioneers in the introduction of self-organized teams. The HR manager of the entire group, on whose watch the introduction of the new corporate forms took place, set up his own business as a management consultant on self-organization and acquired his first orders on the basis of references to the success of his former company.

However, if one had looked backstage at the company, it would have quickly become clear to any observer that, once they had been introduced, the self-organized teams only existed on the show side of the company. The customer- and product-related production islands that had been brought in were quickly dissolved and classic process-oriented departments were reintroduced. Indirect tasks such as personnel planning, order fine-tuning, maintenance, and quality assurance, which had originally been transferred to the competence of the islands, were once again grouped together in central departments. Group spokespersons were once again given hierarchical authority. They became, as the managing director put it, "a little bit" like department heads or shift supervisors. According to the managing director in a confidential conversation, the entire company was on its way "back to the future."

However, it would be premature to describe these group work projects as failures simply because the self-organized teams only exist on the show side. Simply being hailed as a pioneering company for group work had positive effects. Firstly, the management succeeded in gaining important leeway through the group work project. By linking up with the current decentralized production concepts, the managing directors were able to convince the holding companies to make further substantial investments in the loss-making venture. Secondly, the introduction of group work proved to be an additional sales argument and led to an improvement in sales opportunities in the core automotive market.

2.2.4   The Suggestion of Scientificity

At first glance, one would have to assume that scientific legitimization is not necessary for a management fashion. It should be sufficient for the promoters to point out the usefulness and practicability of the solutions that their brainchild provides to fundamental problems in organizations. Ultimately, the question of whether management fashions are useful or not is the dominant factor in anchoring them in organizations.

In science, on the other hand, the focus is on the question of whether a finding is true or false. The question of whether a scientific finding is also useful outside of science is of secondary importance. Scientists address other scientists with their research—at least in specific areas of science. In this respect, the prejudice held by practitioners that researchers make no effort to present their findings in an "understandable" way is justified. As a result, the reference to the fact that a management fashion was conceived in a scientific ivory tower could trigger mistrust among practitioners and raise doubts about its practicability.

At second glance, however, it is noticeable that promoters of a number of management fashions attach importance to the fact that these are backed up by science (cf. Kieser 1997b, p. 58). It is emphasized that the inventors of a fashion are based at a famous university. US universities in particular have developed a branch of business of their own in which practitioners are given professorial titles to transform the university's reputation into financially lucrative training courses for managers, which are at best only loosely linked to the university's scientific standing (for a prototype of this strategy, e.g. MIT's, see Senge 1990 or Scharmer 2009b).

Management bestsellers are embellished with references to great thinkers and great science. To justify their own approach, they point out that a "large number of researchers – including psychologists, philosophers and anthropologists – have closely studied the journey of human consciousness" and have thus developed the foundations for the concept developed for their own evolutionary organizations (Laloux 2014, p. 5).

One reason for the fixation on science in many management fashions could lie in the status anxiety of managers and consultants—at least Andrzej Huczynski suspects as much (Huczynski 2006). While the education of members of established professions such as doctors, lawyers, or theologians is scientifically based and takes place for the most part at universities, the training of managers and consultants has no comparable scientific foundation. This perceived difference in status compared to established professions can lead to managers and consultants being particularly susceptible to scientific explanations for management fashions.

2.3 On the Limits of a Purpose-Driven Approach

The understanding of organizations propagated in management fashions is attractive to managers and consultants on account of its simple, purpose-driven nature. However, it has a fundamental problem: organizations do not function according to such rational planning concepts. This can be seen in the many dilemmas, contradictions, and paradoxes that organizations are confronted with. Organizations need clear objectives, but also a willingness to possibly deviate from defined objectives. It makes sense for employees to identify with processes, but at the same time this identification also hinders any necessary changes. Employee participation can unleash the potential for change, but too much employee involvement makes it more difficult for the organization to focus on dominant goals. Self-organization can be helpful because solutions are developed locally; however, external organization often ensures that any solutions have greater originality. Organizations are faced with the need to create freedom for innovation; however, this creation of buffers often allows organizational slippage to set in. They are dependent on successful learning processes, but successful learning processes are the very things that are responsible for the decline of organizations. This is why avoiding learning can be a sensible strategy.

The fact that different requirements have to be mapped in the organization itself inevitably results in organizations with inconsistent goals and logics. Conflict between the legal department, the research and development department, and the labor policy department over whether a new production process should be introduced is something that cannot be avoided owing to the different environmental reference points of the individual departments involved. The consequence of this orientation of the organization towards a number of different environments—the legal system, the scientific system, the political system—is that, although different environmental requirements can be processed, the organization can no longer undertake an internal rationalization with a view to dealing with just one reference problem.

If you look at the reality, the demands placed on employees are deeply contradictory. On the one hand, they are expected to compete within the organization as "entrepreneurs within the enterprise," while, on the other, they need to be able to cooperate with other employees. Motto: Everyone has to pull together, but only the best prevail. On the one hand, they are expected to go their own way, but, on the other, they must not lose sight of the overall goal of the organization. Motto: Everyone goes their own way, but we are all in the same boat. On the one hand, members of an organization should—if necessary—break rules and regulations imposed from above; on the other hand, however, they should respect the structures laid down by the organization. Motto: Do what you want to, but don't violate any written or unwritten laws. On the one hand, there should be room and scope for lateral thinkers with their creativity and flexibility; on the other hand, the organization's resources should be used as effectively as possible. Motto: Be unorthodox, but don't hinder the standardization of processes in the name of efficiency.

2.3.1   The Proverbs of Management

The organizational theorist and economist Herbert A. Simon (1946, p. 53) was quick to recognize this contradiction in requirements. He drew attention to the fact that the principles of management proclaimed up and down the country function like well-known country proverbs. For every proverb replete with wisdom, a similarly plausible-sounding saying can be found that says the exact opposite. When initiating a relationship, should you follow the maxim "birds of a feather flock together" or the principle that "opposites attract"? Is it the "early bird that catches the worm" or rather the "second mouse that gets the cheese"?

And in the same way, for every rule of thumb put forward by one management consultant, you can extract another rule from a different—even sometimes from the same—management consultant that recommends the exact opposite (see Pfeffer and Sutton 2006, p. 34ff.). Ought one to follow management consultants' plausible recommendation to flatten hierarchies and increase the span of control of individuals, or heed the contrary recommendation and keep the span of control as small as possible in order to ensure the responsiveness of managers, even if this inevitably entails an increase in the number of levels in the hierarchy (cf. Simon 1946, p. 55)? With respect to compliance management, should we view the tendency to break rules as a first step towards "chaos" and use terms such as "management with integrity," "decent leadership," or "honest behavior" to encourage compliance with them, or should we castigate a fixation on compliance with rules as "bureaucratism" and use terms such as "mold breaker" to pay tribute to someone for intelligently ignoring the rulebook (see Kühl 2022, p. 188ff.)?

Much of management literature is built on the principle of folk wisdom. The author of a typical management bestseller picks out one of the many hoary old rules of management, invents stories of organizations that have achieved success by following it, and provides reasons why, in order to survive, each and every organization must abide by the particular rule that they favor. They keep quiet about the fact that organizations may have very good reasons for advocating exactly the opposite rule and may even devise unfriendly names for the opposite principle in order to make their own appear more plausible.

When you read management texts, you are often reminded of books that are read aloud in children's bedrooms every evening. Simple black and white schemes are used—hierarchical external control versus team-based self-control; directives from above versus joint agreements; a purpose-oriented formal structure versus a values-based organizational culture; divided units versus cooperating cells; centralized accountability versus decentralized responsibility; rigid management versus flexible leadership; or thoughtless adaptation versus an agile attitude. Faced with these simple juxtapositions, you don't have to think very hard about which side you are going to identify with.

The advantages of such simple contrasts should not be underestimated, though. You can be sure that the cognitive abilities of the recipients are not overtaxed. Clear tables can be constructed in which the bad can be contrasted with the good and thus a quick consensus established in favor of the right choice. This makes it possible to create easily accessible stories that trace the arduous but highly satisfying path from the bad side to the good. The disadvantage of these simple contrasts, however, is that they have nothing whatever to do with everyday organizational life.

Ambidexterity as a Management Fashion

There is hardly a topic in the field of organization that is not suitable for being taken up in the form of a management fashion. For example, dealing with conflicting requirements in organizations has been seized on and popularized in the concept of ambidexterity. It dishes up the classic question in organizational theory—How can organizations develop new ideas in a creative mode of "exploration" while at the same time benefiting from the efficiency of optimized structures in a mode of "exploitation"?—in an acceptable form for practitioners (Andriopoulos and Lewis 2009; see March 2010). The focus is on how organizations attempt to reconcile contradictory principles within the three dimensions of meaning.

As far as the social dimension is concerned, it has been worked out that people develop skills through their professional training and socialization that are adapted to the different requirements of organizations. Business economists are assumed to have a strong focus on the creative search for suitable means to achieve predetermined goals, while lawyers are seen as experts in the development and interpretation of complex if–then rules. The difference in professional expertise does not have to be seen as a shortcoming, but can be seen as helpful professional diversity in organizations on the basis of the division of labor.

As for the material dimension, it has been shown that all organizations can align their units in accordance with the extent to which they have to deal with uncertainties in the environment. Units that are capable of absorbing uncertainty, such as research, development, human resources and marketing, cushion the contradictory requirements in such a way that the technical core of the organization can be trimmed for efficiency through optimized structures. This means that members of the organization do not have to endure the conflicting requirements themselves, but can concentrate on the mechanism that is central to their own organizational unit (for the classic account, see Thompson 1967).

And as for the time dimension, it should be noted that a central ability of organizations is to recognize when they should focus more on exploration and when they should focus more on exploitation (see March 1991). This can be observed particularly in venture-capital-financed companies that focus on the rapid development of new products and services during a boom in the financial market, without worrying whether these are likely to yield only short-term profits, and then, when the financial market collapses, try almost in a panic to secure their liquidity by establishing efficient structures and selling off their discoveries to at least cover their costs.

However, this interesting perspective on the structure of organizations is often obscured by the fact that "ambidexterity" is often reduced to a personal characteristic. In modern organizations, so management literature often has it, people have to be able to act "ambidextrously," i.e. to be able to work in both the creative "exploration" and the efficient "exploitation" mode. The fact that these personal skills are not necessary at all, because the organization itself can ensure that there are structures in place to ensure ambidexterity, is overlooked.

2.3.2   The Inevitability of Unintended Side Effects

So far, so good. However, proclaiming the reconciliation of irreconcilables obscures a central effect of decision making in organizations—namely that every decision made in every organization, whatever its many positive effects, will inevitably bring with it problematic side effects. The consistent streamlining of processes means that there is no protective buffer against extraordinary events. Demanding and enforcing adherence to rules means that organizations are unable to react to events as they occur. In short: no matter what you decide, you can safely assume that there will be unwanted side effects.

This means that whenever a decision is reached after lengthy deliberation, there would have been good reasons for deciding to do the exact opposite. A clear strategy may have been decided on, but perhaps it might have been a better idea not to be too specific in view of rapidly changing environmental conditions. Decision makers may have followed quality management's recommendation "First time right counts" on the basis of sound arguments, only to realize that they might just as plausibly have chosen "Just do it, and then keep figuring out how to do it better" as their guide.

2.3.3   The Cyclical Nature of Management Fashions

The proverbial nature of management concepts explains why a management fashion can establish itself as the dominant model in organizational fields, only to be quickly replaced by another model. Management fashions do not disappear from one moment to the next, however; they actually tend to die out quite slowly. One reason for this is that management fashions are not static, but exhibit a considerable degree of minor variation.

On the one hand, organizations need to adapt to current developments; at the same time, they must not give the impression that they are merely copying others. According to the popular saying in management, those who only ever follow in the footsteps of others leave no traces themselves. At the end of the day, uniqueness cannot be created with a photocopier. Advocates of a management style therefore do not copy it one-to-one, but change it slightly in order to set their own stamp on it. Following a principle of "imitation plus" in the process of being adopted, a management style is constantly developed further through small adjustments (see Kühl 2020, p. 179ff.).

Ultimately, management fashions are no different from fashions in clothing. There too minor changes are made within a dominant trend. Within a trend for short skirts, these can become more and more close-fitting, they may be cut differently, different fabrics may be used. These variations not only allow different trendsetters to make their mark within a fashion, they also help to ensure that fashions do not wear themselves out too quickly (for more information on dress fashions, see J. W. G. Lowe and E. D. Lowe 1982).

But at some point, despite all the variance, every fashion will have exhausted its potential. Just as with clothing fashions, all variations within a trend will have been tried at some point. The effect in management fashions is that all the derivatives of an organizational concept have already been brought forward and applauded once. The degree of saturation is so high that the market demands something fundamentally new. The management fashion disappears and is replaced by another.

The cyclical nature of management fashions may seem sobering. It shows that there are no convincing reasons for the self-assurance with which management concepts are propagated. Enthusiasm for a management concept is an exercise in self-delusion, as becomes obvious when the fashion fades away, if not before. But despite all this, it may still be functional to use management fashions in change processes.

3

The Use of Management Fashions in Change Processes

By their nature, management fashions are very similar to religions. A path is promised by which work—and, more broadly, life—can once again come to have meaning. Principles are praised that can be used to enable one to reach new levels of consciousness. Catastrophes are prophesied if one does not commit oneself to the new world of thought. What is promised is the salvation not only of the individual, but of the whole world (according to the analyses in, for example, Furnham 2004, p. 4; Collins 2020, p. 135ff.).

The reference to religions is already visible in the use of language. There is talk of the "seven deadly sins" of management. Management principles are flagged up as the "ten commandments" of the organization. Managers do not hesitate to call themselves "chief evangelists" vis-à-vis their employees (on the religious charge in management fashions, see Ellis and Tissen 2003).

Critics pick up on the religious nature of management fashions and complain that their advocates behave like followers of a cult, who count themselves as belonging to the elect who understand how organizations should function in this day and age. The cultivation of a management concept at seminars and conferences is reminiscent of a "spiritual practice" in which the participants put themselves into a

S. Kühl, *Making use of Management Fashions*,
https://doi.org/10.1007/978-3-032-09265-6_3

spiritual state (in this connection, see, for example, Greatbatch and Clark 2005, p. 12ff.; Huczynski 2006, p. 206ff.; Alvesson 2013, p. 130ff.)

What is overlooked in this criticism, however, is that management concepts fulfil important functions in organizations precisely because of their almost religious charge. In short: it is precisely because management fashions have great similarities with religions, that they can play a central role in organizational change processes.

3.1   The Difficulty of Change in Organizations

Organizations are faced with the challenge of having to make decisions under conditions of high uncertainty (see Luhmann 1964, p. 173). If it were clear to everyone what the right course of action is, there would be no need to make a decision because one would only have to do what is obvious anyway. Decisions are therefore always determinations made in situations in which one cannot be sure whether what one has decided is correct. Every decision taken in an organization is therefore inevitably risky. It can always turn out later that a different decision would have been better after all (for the basics, see Luhmann 1993, p. 287ff.).

3.1.1   Uncertainties in Decision Making in Organizations

People make decisions that later turn out to be wrong outside of organizations as well as within them. Choosing a particular place to go for a vacation can turn out to be a mistake if its attractiveness has led to it becoming overcrowded. One may come to regret the choice of a spouse made in a phase of acute infatuation if, over the years, he or she displays unexpectedly rigid behavior patterns and the argument about the infamous toothpaste tube becomes a permanent point of conflict. The decision to have children may turn out in retrospect to have been mistaken if one underestimated how nerve-wracking parenting can be. Decision making in organizations, however, comes with a number of aggravating conditions.

Firstly, there is permanent uncertainty in organizations as to whether their structure is still appropriate in the face of changing environmental conditions. If everything might be different tomorrow, organizations' current self-definitions may well seem risky. Who can guarantee that what used to be original ideas or efficient established routines will not be the first nail in your company's coffin in the foreseeable future? To put it in terms of systems theory: previously successful forms of uncertainty absorption are themselves becoming uncertain.

Secondly, there is often an overload of information when it comes to decision making in organizations. While it used to be difficult for organizations to obtain information, today they are overloaded with it. Instead of a lack of information, there is more of a threat of an "information blackout"—a kind of epileptic reaction on the part of the organization to an information overload. In order to prevent this blackout, organizations are forced to select more or less arbitrarily from the available information when making decisions. In view of the frequently contradictory nature of information, it is often impossible to know until much later whether a decision has been made on the basis of information that is actually correct.

Thirdly, the problem is exacerbated by the fact that organizations can become afraid of falling behind other organizations through contact with them (Huczynski 1993a, p. 450). Organizations always operate in fields that are shaped by other organizations (see DiMaggio and Powell 1983, p. 148). Even if they are not necessarily in direct competition with these organizations, they compare themselves with them and are compared with them. There is competition—albeit often unspoken—as to which organization in a field can best master the challenges. An organization can never be sure how it will fare in this competition.

3.1.2 Reducing Uncertainty and Responsibility in Decision Making

Organizations could, ultimately, rely on themselves to make decisions. The understanding of problems in an organization is usually precise enough for the necessary know-how to be available to assess alternatives. In an organization the members know where communication problems between departments come from and how they can be resolved, which routines do not work as planned, and which people are in the right positions and which are not. With this knowledge alone, organizations should be able to weigh up the advantages and disadvantages of different alternatives and make decisions on that basis.

The problem, however, is that someone has to take responsibility for all decisions taken under conditions of uncertainty. If it turns out that, all things considered, a decision must be perceived as "wrong" for the organization, this often signals the start of a search for culprits. The people who made the decision at the time are identified and can therefore be held responsible for it (see Luhmann 1964, p. 174ff.).

This is why organizations develop a variety of strategies to reduce responsibility for a decision. In many cases, heavyweight expert consulting firms are brought in not because of the quality of their consulting services, but because responsibility for decisions can be outsourced to them. The establishment of collective decision-making bodies in the form of self-organized teams reduces the individual responsibility of team members. The involvement of as many people as possible through participatory change processes makes it more difficult for any individual to be held solely responsible for a decision.

Given the risks involved in decision making, management fashions play an important role. Managers can justify decisions by saying that all organizations are currently following a trend. When redesigning an organization, they can point out that this is seen as the only way to deal with changing demands on the basis of the management concepts currently in circulation. One can justify one's own approach by imitating the structures of organizations that are being spoken of in the management press as particularly progressive and are therefore considered to be particularly successful. In short, management fashions serve as safety surrogates in such a situation. They reduce the risk of being held accountable for decisions because you have only done what everyone else has been doing.

3.2   Creating a Willingness to Change

Confrontation with management fashions initially increases complexity and therefore also uncertainty in organizations. They trigger irritation in organizations because things have to be done differently than before. This initially increases the decision-making options in the organization because another option opens up alongside the status quo. However, management fashions immediately reduce complexity again because they offer a stringent, coherent concept.

3.2.1 Reducing Complexity Through Management Methods

Various design principles and management tools are combined in a package and then adorned with an impressive label such as "total quality management," "lean management," or "agile operating system" (on the concept of the package form, see Gill and Whittle 1992, p. 282). The illusion here is that the management of an organization only has to unpack this package to be able to benefit directly from its contents (see Huczynski 2006, p. 112).

The suggestion behind the package format is that a management concept can be purchased in its entirety. Just as you can delete outdated software and replace it with new standard software, you can also, according to the sales promise, delete the organization's old operating system and replace it with a new management system. As with standard software, a new management system will require a few adjustments, but you know roughly what you are getting. For organizations, this promise is an enormous relief if it has to make decisions during a change process.

3.2.2 Elimination of Unwanted Side Effects

However, every "problem solution" inevitably entails "solution problems" (Luhmann 1964, p. 382). The more detailed thought is given to the consequences of a particular decision, the more critical the light in which the decision taken will be viewed. It is only when the possible consequences of a reform are extensively and prominently discussed that certain concerns are aroused and spread within the organization.

Management fashions help to conceal any "solution problems." They create a simple choice between two alternatives—one that is not very convincing at first glance and one that is very convincing (Brunsson 1989, p. 189ff.). The current status quo of an organization is not very attractive because its weak points have been identified over time. By contrast, the organizational principles propagated in a management fashion are attractive because they have not yet had to prove themselves in the everyday reality of the organization.

Many organizations believe that people are motivated to follow a well-thought-out decision on the basis of their own rationality. The more intensively set up such a decision-making process has been, the more likely it is that the members of the organization will feel encouraged to implement the decision. However, the opposite is often the case: the more thought is given to the consequences of a particular decision, the more critically the decision is viewed. People subscribe to notions of "decision rationality," but disregard whether there is sufficient energy left at the end to make the decision effective (Brunsson 1985, p. 59ff.).

Management fashions, on the other hand, can increase the "rationality of action" in organizations because they encourage people to do things differently (Brunsson 2007, p. 68f.). The problematic consequences of a favored option are systematically ignored. Success stories of pioneering organizations are retold without taking the trouble to look behind the scenes. Orientation by management fashion does not correspond in any way to the familiar ideas of rational decision making, but it has the advantage that the decision is sold as unproblematic and can therefore have a motivating effect.

3.3   The Opportunities Offered by the Ambiguity of Management Fashions

The attraction of many management fashions for practitioners lies in a mixture of simplicity and ambiguity (see, in the first instance, Clark and Salaman 1996, p. 85ff.). The simplicity of most management fashions gives the impression of spontaneous plausibility. A company that allows its employees to act as entrepreneurs within the company seems more appealing than one that systematically stifles its employees' initiative through bureaucratic regulations. A company that is based on the model of a tent that can be moved at any time is more attractive than one that is based on the model of a palace. An organization that presents itself as a network evokes more sympathy than one that presents itself as centralized (all examples in Kieser 1997b, p. 58f.).

At the same time, however, many management fashions are characterized by a high degree of ambiguity (for an early account, see Bendix 1956, p. 342). The consequence for many of them is that it remains unclear how they are to be implemented in detail (Miller and Hartwick 2002, p. 26f.; Miller et al. 2004, p. 12). Although the recipe-like descriptions of the approach, the examples of pioneering organizations, and the chapters on implementation suggest immediate practicability, management is left with a certain amount of uncertainty as to exactly how everything is to be put into practice (Micklethwait and Wooldrige 1996, p. 83; Collins 2020, p. 20). This is precisely where organizations have considerable scope to shape things for themselves.

The Charm of a Ready-Made Concept

Why It Can Make Sense for a Medium-Sized Company to Purchase a Ready-Made Organizational Concept for Several Million Euros

Agile methods are easy to introduce at team level, when tasks are clearly defined tasks and there are fewer than a dozen employees. If a team can work largely autonomously on the development of a product, it is comparatively easy to align this with customer needs via the appointment of a "product owner" to organize the development process via one or two-week sprints and carry out short-term coordination via daily "stand-ups." It always becomes difficult when a development task requires a large number of teams that need to be coordinated with one another.

Consulting firms have therefore developed concepts that are intended to make it possible to transfer the agile concept, which has been successful at the level of individual teams, to the entire organization. "Scaling up" is the magic word used to describe this process—scaling-up agile forms of work. The promise made by consulting firms to their potential clients is simple. We have a toolbox for you that not only contains proven, immediately applicable tools, but these tools are also all precisely coordinated with each other.

These concepts combine everything that is currently *en vogue* in management discourse. Methods such as scrums, kanbans, backlogs, key performance indicators, portfolios, and value streams are used, enriched with concepts such as customer-centricity, design thinking, continuous exploration, and iterations. Popular role descriptions such as product owner, business owner, epic owner, scrum manager, product manager, system architect, enterprise architects, and team coach are also included. Of course, the usual buzzwords such as lean-agile mindset, core values, visions, objectives and key results, artificial intelligence, shared service, and community of practice also figure. The visual representation of these concepts is similar to popular hidden-object pictures, in which you can always discover something new among the confusion.

A French mechanical engineering company with ten thousand employees is suffering from the fact that its individual development processes are becoming increasingly complex and difficult to coordinate. They are therefore considering introducing one of the standardized agility models. Before introducing it, the responsible division managers decide to have a brief analysis carried out to determine whether the complex and costly introduction of such a model makes sense.

This analysis shows that only two elements in the scaled agile framework are relevant for accelerating product development. The first central lever is that individual product developments should be driven by autonomous product development units. This should lead to an acceleration because the product developers no longer have to work on several development projects at the same time, but can concentrate on a single one in an "agile release train." The second lever is the fact that the company's seven central development projects take a day every four weeks and meet up to present their respective development progress to each other and synchronize upcoming developments.

Because the other one hundred and twelve starting points for the agile framework are irrelevant for increasing development speed, the organizational analysts recommend not introducing the agile framework as a whole, but focusing instead on the introduction of autonomous product development teams and the timing of the respective development steps that the teams are to take. The argument is that consistent work on the two central levers will ensure success in product development, whereas the introduction of the entire comprehensive framework would lead to loss of focus. There is a concern that, without focusing on the two levers, the organization will not have the strength to assign all the employees exclusively to one development project and to bring the various development projects into the rhythm of four-week sprints.

The management rejects this proposal from the organizational analysts and decides to introduce the entire scaled agile framework for several million. The argument is that there are too many different views, too many different understandings of processes, and too many isolated solutions in the company so that a centrally defined framework is needed. At first glance, this idea contradicts the idea of agility, because the change process is not incremental and instead the new structure for the development organization is introduced with a long-term master plan. However, the management's decision has its own rationality. The company is so frayed in the development process, the micropolitical distortions are so pronounced, that the organization is not even capable of pragmatic work on the two structural levers. It seems to need a scaled framework that can be sold as an industry standard in order to force the units into a uniform structure by means of a "package solution" and to overcome resistance with the argument of a supposed best practice.

3.3.1 The Difference Between Values and Programs

The design options become clear when a distinction is made between values and programs. Values—think of such formulations such as "We organize ourselves in agile teams," "We work in a self-determined way in a co-creation mode," or "We are sustainable in our actions"—represent behavioral expectations, but do not determine which actions can be expected in a specific situation. Due to their abstract nature, values have "high chances of consensus," but leave open how they are to be implemented in concrete terms (Luhmann 1972, p. 88f.).

Programs, on the other hand, are rules for making the right decisions. They define the specific expectations that organizational members must adhere to. The point about programs is that—unlike values—it is possible to identify with certainty whether they have been carried out correctly or not. Whether customers have been treated like kings is open to multiple interpretations. Whether 5% new customers were acquired in 1 year or sales increased by 16% can be determined unequivocally.

The Creative Handling of the Requirement for a More Agile Approach in a Japanese Electronics Group

The management board of a Japanese electronics group decides that agile forms of organization should be introduced throughout the company. This is based on positive experiences in the electronic tools division, where development times have been significantly reduced by means of stable teams using sprints. The hope is to achieve similar effects in the automotive technology, building technology, and household appliances divisions by introducing agile forms of working.

A program will be set up in which all divisions in the group will be encouraged to implement agilization measures. These are to be implemented not only in product development, but also in purchasing, production, sales, and services. Based on positive experiences in one area, agility with fixed teams and structuring via sprints is seen not only as a recipe for success in product development, but also as a sensible principle for adoption by all functions within the Group.

The head of services in the area of household appliances, which has several hundred employees, is faced with the challenge of implementing this agilization program prescribed from above and reporting on progress to management. However, the success of her division depends primarily on stable processes at the interface with the customer. Customers who have problems with their dishwasher or washing machine need to know that they can reach a contact for their problem immediately and that a service employee will be on site within 24 hours. This requires the organization to be programmed with precise if-then rules, which is in stark contrast to the goal-oriented principles of agile working methods in product development.

Instead of burdening the group's top management, which is driven by the currently fashionable agility model, with the inconsistency inherent in their group-wide reorganization project, the head of the service division decides to run her already planned project to further standardize service performance under the label of agility. She uses the vocabulary popular with top management to spruce up the language describing her own project, which she has been planning with her employees for a long time. Because top management does not have the time to deal with the details of individual reorganization projects in the divisions, this pragmatic approach to the requirements of agilization goes through without a hitch. In the end, the service manager succeeds in positioning her project, which is based on further standardization, as a showcase for agility.

Management fashions always suggest that they not only consist of nice-sounding catalogs of values, but also show how organizational structures can be implemented in concrete terms. They cannot do without this because very few practitioners in organizations will be interested in reading a pure catalog of values. Therefore, when management fashions are being propagated, it is vital to convey the impression that they are directly effective in practice. But this is just a simple sales argument used to conceal the high degree of abstraction in a management concept. And that is actually a good thing—because only a high degree of abstraction can create opportunities for of the people who shape organizations to take action on their own behalf.

3.3.2 Interpretability as an Opportunity

Managers can take much of the legitimizing effect of a high-profile management concept with them into their reform projects, while at the same time addressing the specific pain points in the organization and looking for pragmatic solutions (for a compact presentation of the points below, see Sturdy et al. 2019, p. 7). It is possible to benefit from the popularity of a very generally formulated management idea without being restricted by it in one's choice of options for action (for the use of interpretability, see Reay et al. 2013). Managers are not puppets led by management gurus, but play a central role in the translation of management concepts into practice (see Spyridonidis et al. 2016).

This decoupling of the basic principles from their concrete implementation can be observed in the use of various management methods (see Guillén 1994, p. 281ff.). Thanks to the success of Japanese companies, lean management was for some time considered a promising recipe for reducing assembly times, increasing quality, and cutting costs. But even in the American and European subsidiaries of Japanese companies, the principles were not implemented as originally intended. Although the same terminology was used as at the parent company, the subsidiaries ultimately did what they themselves considered appropriate (on the significance of the Japan myth, see Kühl 2020, p. 80ff.).

The decoupling can go to the point where structural changes are implemented under the label of a current management fashion, which, on closer inspection, run entirely counter to its intentions. Organizations decide to implement an agile form of organization by hiring on a long-term basis an expert consulting firm that has prevailed in an elaborate tendering process. Although this long-term commitment contradicts the idea of an agile, step-by-step, incremental approach, it relieves top management of the need to constantly reconsider how it should proceed. Alternatively, organizations use the guiding principle of self-organization to hold out the prospect of greater decentralization of decision-making processes, but by removing several levels of middle management, ultimately enforce greater centralization of decision making at the top of the organization.

This form of decoupling between propagated basic principles and concrete implementation requires ingenuity in the presentation of one's own approach. The introduction of new departments, each with their own rationalities, as part of a reorganization under the pretext of agility can be

The Concealed Matrix

How an Automotive Supplier Unintentionally Reintroduced a Management Concept That Was Thought to be Obsolete
A few decades ago, the matrix organization was seen as a solution to central organizational problems. In contrast to an organizational model based on the functions of development, purchasing, production, marketing, and sales, the matrix structure was intended to ensure that, in addition to a focus on functions, an orientation toward a particular product and region could also come into play. To this end, a structure was created in which employees based their decisions on functional requirements but with equal emphasis on regional and product-based perspectives. The hope was that this would make it possible to balance out the conflict of aims arising out of functional, regional, and product-specific requirements.

However, it quickly became apparent that the introduction of a matrix structure leads to an enormous increase in complexity in the organization. In a three-dimensional matrix, employees face three superiors, to each of whom they are accountable (for a critical early account, see Gulick 1937, p. 9). These superiors are rarely in agreement because their positions require them to adopt different perspectives. In some cases, the negotiations between them lead to an intelligent balancing of the demands of all three dimensions. In many cases, however, there is a blockage because it is difficult to reach any decision at all in a matrix structure.

This effect has led to massive criticism of the matrix structure concept. According to its critics, introducing a matrix structure is like playing basketball, tennis, and soccer on the same field with the same players at the same time (see Bogdanich and Forsythe 2022, p. 190f.). Consequently, for a while, it was claimed that "excellent organizations" are characterized by the fact that they consistently avoid matrix structures and instead concentrate responsibility in autonomous units (Peters and Waterman 1982, p. 49).

The result is that hardly any managers or consultants now stand up and aggressively propagate the introduction of a matrix structure. To do so would be to show themselves to be outdated, because they are clinging to a concept whose negative aspects are now well known. Because of this reputational loss, researchers who do not conduct empirical research into organizations but generate their findings from an analysis of management discourse assume that matrix structures have largely disappeared from organizations.

However, things have actually developed differently. In many cases, matrix structures become established not as a result of the concept being aggressively propagated by management, rather they creep in unintentionally through the adaptation of a currently fashionable management concept. The introduction of matrix structures is often not the result of a conscious decision in their favor, but rather as an unintended side effect of a reorganization project driven by a management trend.

The management of a US automotive supplier decides to introduce a process organization. The functional organizational structure is retained with its division into development, purchasing, production, marketing, and sales, but cross-functional process control is introduced in parallel in the process organization. The hope is to consistently align all value creation processes in the company with customer benefits. By precisely defining the interfaces to upstream and downstream processes, the aim is to increase quality, shorten delivery times, and speed up market launches.

In order to set up the process organization, roles are defined that have responsibility for processes. On the one hand, "process leads" are designated, who are intended to have a more coordinating role in describing processes, and on the other hand, "process owners" are appointed higher up in the hierarchy, whose job is to make binding decisions with regard to standard processes in the organization. Because the organization itself is not yet sure how far it wants to take the process organization, employees take on tasks as "process leads" or "process owners" in addition to their positions in the functional organization or their responsibility for particular products.

Without intending to, the company has added another dimension to its already complex matrix structure. In addition to its orientation toward functions such as purchasing, development, production, marketing, and sales and the company's six central product lines, process orientation has been introduced as a third dimension. However, because the process organization was sold as an alternative to the existing matrix structure, management is not even in a position to discuss the topic of process organization from the point of view of its further complicating the matrix structure.

Because the management itself is unclear during the introduction process as to whether process orientation should be the dominant dimension, whether it should be on an equal footing with the functions and product lines, or whether the process owners should merely take on a coordinating role, the organization is blocked by negotiation processes. The focus on customer benefit has degenerated into a strategic argument used by process owners and process leads to strengthen their own position in the organization vis-à-vis the functional department heads and product line managers. In fact, the customer has been pushed further out of focus because the organization is primarily concerned with itself in the matrix.

linguistically concealed by no longer calling these departments departments, but calling them chapters, tribes, or communities instead. The introduction of a new hierarchical level as part of a project to increase resilience, which makes sense for pragmatic reasons, can be kept hidden by not showing it in the official organization chart. As an advocate of "pure doctrine", one may be annoyed by this creative interpretation of a management fashion, but one can also consider it a clever procedure by a management oriented towards pragmatic solutions.

3.4 Praise and Blame for Ignorance

The element of forgetfulness and forgettability in management discourse means that structural principles regularly experience a renaissance after one or two decades (see Barley and Kunda 1992). Organizations that removed several levels of middle management during the lean management phase, but then reintroduced hierarchical levels in order to reduce management breakdowns, may reactivate the idea of self-organized teams under the label of agility and reduce hierarchical levels again. Organizations that threaten to suffocate under their own bureaucracy use organizational culture hype to reduce the level of detail in the formalization of their rules and regulations, but then find that extensive deformalization causes internal complexity to explode. They then use the enthusiasm for process organizations to introduce new formal rules, only to reduce the degree of formalization again under the slogan of flexibilization.

What are the consequences of this cyclical nature in the use of management concepts?

3.4.1   The Risk of Using Management Methods

When presenting management concepts, sporadic reference is made to previously existing concepts, but these are not based on a systematic accumulation of knowledge. Advocates of management fashions have to ignore what has already been considered and tried, because otherwise it would be impossible to present their ideas as something new. A management consultant's announcement that, after careful consideration, has come to the conclusion that the now almost one-hundred-year-old concept of management by objectives is the best thing for organizations would hardly attract any attention. She has to reactivate the idea under new terminology such as objectives and key results and act as if it is a fundamentally new development compared to all previously existing ideas on managing organizations by means of target agreements.

The dramatization of novelty in the propagation of management fashions conceals the fact that all the principles for structuring organizations have been known for well over a hundred years and have been tried out in practice in different variations (see Drucker 2016, p. 19; for the example of organizational culture, see Lammers 1987). The upshot is that we know exactly what effects specific structural changes in organizations have—the insourcing and outsourcing of services from the organization, the centralization or decentralization of decision making, supervisors as members of teams or as leaders outside of teams, rewarding achievements by individuals or crediting the entire organization. The effects may vary in detail in organizations because the individual measures are combined differently, but precise statements can be made about the intended and unintended consequences of a specific structural measure.

One of the achievements of organizational science has certainly been to compile and condense this knowledge about the effects of structural changes. Even if organizational scientists write primarily for their academic colleagues, practitioners can draw helpful information from their articles and books on the intended and unintended consequences of planned structural changes. But in many cases, this recourse is unnecessary because the knowledge is available from experienced practitioners. Members of organizations have often gone through so many reorganizations in their lives that they can predict the effects of a reform if it is stripped of the usual verbal tinsel and reduced to its organizational and structural foundations.

3.4.2 Memory and Forgetfulness

Those responsible for reform processes must consider carefully whether they want to make knowledge of past reforms available within the organization or whether they want to obscure it by using management fashions. After all, knowledge of bad experiences in the past, unavoidable unwanted side effects and possible similarly attractive alternatives always threatens to take motivation away from a reform process that has been set in motion by parasitizing on a management fashion. Consideration has to be given in all three dimensions of meaning to how one wants to make use of management fashions' capacity to obscure.

In the factual dimension, organizations should consider whether they should rely more on concepts that attempt to spell out in detail how an organization should align itself or on open, interpretable concepts. The advantage of management concepts that define the formal structural foundations down to the last detail is that they relieve management of the need to think and decide on a large number of points. The disadvantage is that it is difficult to move away from the concept when its side effects become increasingly clear in practice; the first pioneering organizations fail and the criticism becomes increasingly fierce. Management fashions such as the learning organization, the knowledge-based company, or the self-organized enterprise are so general that almost anything can be done under those labels. These very vaguely defined management fashions therefore do not disappear so quickly, but lose their appeal over time because at some point they have worn out their usefulness as a badge for reforms in an organization.

In the social dimension, the question arises as to which members of the organization are more likely to be inspired with enthusiasm for reform with the aid of a management fad and which should be encouraged to think critically about possible organizational forms. Because advocates of management fashions with their usual dramatization of novelties obscure knowledge of the effects of structural changes, it can be useful as part of the organization's own risk management to activate this knowledge at least selectively. Small groups of long-serving employees can be set up to compile experiences with similar reform projects in the past, or smaller-scale expert reports can be commissioned to anticipate the effects of a planned structural change on the basis of interviews with interested members of the organization. Whether or not this knowledge should then be widely shared within the organization should be carefully considered, however, as loss of momentum is a constant threat.

In the time dimension, it is important to make use of a management fashion as close to its zenith as possible. A management concept generates most momentum for a reform process when the first organizations report on their successes with it and the public starts to take note. If a management fashion is only just emerging, it will not possess sufficient legitimacy because very few people are familiar with the concept. When the significance of a management fashion starts to wane, it can even be counterproductive to run a reform process under that flag, because the first articles about the failure of pioneering organizations will be appearing and this will inevitably generate critical questions within your own organization.

If a management fashion is in decline, an organization should preferably not be associated with it. But the decline of a management fashion does not mean that its structural principle will disappear for good. Forgettability in management discourse means that an organizational structural principle will experience a renaissance after one or two decades. The structural principle will then suddenly be *en vogue* again—albeit under a new name.

4

Working with Management Fashions: A Conclusion

It is understandable that practitioners who identify with a management concept should become annoyed with this functionalist perspective. Practitioners, according to the critics, would stimulate discussion with new proposals, while the only thing that it would occur to the theorists to do would be to laboriously bring up their "heavy guns," position them, and then fire at targets that they can only vaguely make out. The theorists would meticulously compile a list of "what is claimed where and why it does not 'fit together'," what is "untested or even untestable," "unrealistic," "unsystematic," or "lacking in theory," but would never bother to develop a concept that could be put into practice (Neuberger 1996, p. 277).

But—it's a legitimate question—aren't organizational theorists with their abstract models just as subject to cyclical fashions as the proponents of management concepts? Isn't what is called organizational science "made" in very much the same way as management fashions (Neuberger 1996, p. 278)? Isn't system-theory-based organizational sociology, with its ordering schemes that make up the meta-structure matrix, a concept that is simply in vogue and will be replaced by other, fresher approaches in the foreseeable future?

© The Author(s), under exclusive license to Springer Nature Switzerland AG 2026
S. Kühl, *Making use of Management Fashions*,
https://doi.org/10.1007/978-3-032-09265-6_4

4.1 The Difference Is a Failure to Make Common Cause with a Good Cause

It would be naïve to assume that science is not also subject to certain fashions and trends. Thinking styles develop in science that determine which problems are considered relevant in a community of researchers and which approaches are used to find solutions. In fact, it is not possible to deviate from these dominant thinking styles because they cannot be processed within science (for an early discussion, see Fleck 1935). In scientific research, there is talk of a "paradigm" that determines thinking in a discipline over a longer period of time (see Kuhn 1962; and, for a more intensive treatment, Feyerabend 1975; Feyerabend 1978).

If you look at how organizational theories are made and diffused, you cannot avoid the impression that they are not so different from the construction and diffusion of management concepts (according to Bort and Kieser 2011, p. 672; likewise for economic theories Bronfenbrenner 1966, p. 538ff. and for legal theories Sunstein 2001, p. 1259ff.). In organizational theory, too, there is competition between concepts, with one approach sometimes dominating for a time without anyone knowing exactly why. There, too, people attempt to make a name for themselves with innovations, but in so doing so, they have to take great care to ensure that they retain connectivity. Despite scholars making every effort to create theories that are as complex as possible, you sometimes get the impression that these are ultimately just metaphors that don't seem all that different from those used in management concepts. Organizational theorists also sometimes come across as "storytellers" who, like management gurus, are busy developing an interesting and consistent story (cf. Kieser 1997a, p. 243f.). So it is possible to get the impression that the academic journals that specialize in organization theory are being filled with more and more useless stuff (at least this was the impression left on Starbuck 2009, p. 109ff.). Similarly, organizational theory often works with such vague concepts on topics such as strategy, leadership, and institutions that it is difficult to grasp them (cf. Alvesson and Blom 2022, p. 63ff.).

One might take these characteristics as an opportunity to fundamentally question the scientific nature of organizational theories. If organizational theories and management concepts differ so little in their susceptibility to fashions and trends, there is no reason why people who knock together organizational theories should look down condescendingly on the constructors of management concepts. From this perspective, in fact, receptiveness to fashions and trends in organizational theory can be seen as not so bad, because it allows organizational scholars to free themselves at least a little from the existing theoretical and methodological corset and thus develop a certain urge to innovate (Abrahamson 2009, p. 238).

Despite all the structural similarities between practice-oriented management concepts and organizational science approaches, there is one key difference. The proponents of management concepts always favor a particular form of organizational structure. They find flat hierarchies better than steep ones, decentralization better than centralization, self-organization better than external organization, revolutionary change better than status quo orientation—or sometimes vice versa. In any case, they provide an answer to the question of how organizations should be designed in order to become more innovative, more efficient, more employee-friendly, and more environmentally conscious. In contrast to the advocates of management concepts, organizational theorists do not take a concrete position on what structure

an organization should adopt. They do not take up causes—
not even good ones.

4.2   For a Pragmatic Approach
to Management Fashions

Advocates and supporters of a management concept can,
with good reason, see a functionalist approach to management fashions as a provocation. Instead of believing the
promise that a management concept will make an organization more effective, more efficient, and more innovative,
the concept is initially assumed to have only a useful legitimizing effect on the show side, which can form a protective
framework for reforms. Instead of assuming that a management concept can achieve immediate effectiveness in the
organization, a loose coupling of the show, formal, and informal sides is assumed, so that almost anything can be
done in an organization under the banner of a management
concept.

It is tempting for practitioners to identify with a management concept. It is possible to deal productively with everyday frustrations by committing to something that is presented as an alternative to the familiar hierarchical and
overformalized structures based on division of labor that are
typical of large organizations. You see yourself as part of a
movement that is not only concerned with making organizations more innovative and efficient, but also with making
employees more satisfied. You develop a sense of community with other people who are fighting the same battle to
make organizations more flexible, creative, and agile.

At the same time, you have to be aware that you are con-
siderably limiting the range of decisions when you commit
to a management concept. Consultants who see business

process re-engineering as the solution to everyone's organizational problems risk overlooking the benefits of the functional division of organizations. Employees who, as scrum masters and agile coaches, are enthusiastic about an incremental approach risk overlooking the fact that there may be projects for which long-term planning using detailed specifications may be a sensible approach. If the only tool you have is a hammer—so the saying goes—you tend to see every problem as a nail.

There is a lot to be said for using the entire toolbox as manager, employee, or consultant. There are only a few dozen design principles in organizations: increasing or decreasing the number of levels in a hierarchy, positioning supervisors within or outside teams, giving supervisors larger or smaller spans of control, centralizing or decentralizing decision-making power, management by objectives or based on if–then programs—to name just a few of the most obvious ones. If practitioners can learn anything from organizational scientists, it is that it makes sense to remain open to the entire spectrum of elements of organizational design.

This does not mean that management fashions should be ignored. On the contrary—it makes sense to develop a feel for current trends in order to initiate discourse in organizations and legitimize change projects that have been planned for a long time with a fresh vocabulary. So it is possible to use management fashions productively in organizations— you just shouldn't believe in them too strongly.

References

Abrahamson, Eric. 1996. "Management Fashion." Academy of Management Review 21: 254–85.

Abrahamson, Eric. 2009. "Necessary Conditions for the Study of Fads and Fashions in Science." Scandinavian Journal of Management 5: 235–39.

Alvesson, Mats. 2013. The Triumph of Emptiness: Consumption, Higher Education, and Work Organization. Oxford, New York: Oxford University Press.

Alvesson, Mats, and Martin Blom. 2022. "The Hegemonic Ambiguity of Big Concepts in Organization Studies." Human Relations 75: 58–86.

Andriopoulos, Constantine, and Marianne W. Lewis. 2009. "Exploitation-Exploration Tensions and Organizational Ambidexterity: Managing Paradoxes of Innovation." Organization Science 20 (4): 696–717.

Aspers, Patrik. 2005. Markets in Fashion: A Phenomenological Approach. London: Routledge.

Barley, Stephen R., and Gideon Kunda. 1992. "Design and Devotion: Surges of Rational and Normative Ideologies of

© The Editor(s) (if applicable) and The Author(s), under exclusive license to Springer Nature Switzerland AG 2026
S. Kühl, *Making use of Management Fashions*,
https://doi.org/10.1007/978-3-032-09265-6

Control in Managerial Discourse." Administrative Science Quarterly 37: 363–99.

Barley, Stephen R., and Gideon Kunda. 2004. Gurus, Hired Guns and Warm Bodies: Itinerant Experts in a Knowledge Economy. Princeton: Princeton University Press.

Beck, Kent, Mike Beedle, Arie van Bennekum, Alistair Cockburn, Ward Cunningham, Martin Fowler, James Grenning et al. 2001. "Manifesto for Agile Software Development." https://agilemanifesto.org/.

Bendix, Reinhard. 1956. Work and Authority in Industry. New York: John Wiley.

Blumer, Herbert. 1969. "Fashion: From Class Differentiation to Collective Selection." The Sociological Quarterly 10: 275–91.

Bogdanich, Walt, and Michael Forsythe. 2022. When Mckinsey Comes to Town: The Hidden Influence of the World's Most Powerful Consulting Firm. With the assistance of M. Forsythe. New York: Knopf Doubleday.

Bort, Suleika. 2015. "Turning a Management Innovation into a Management Panacea: Management Ideas, Concepts, Fashions, Practices and Theoretical Concepts." In Örtenblad 2015, 35–56.

Bort, Suleika, and Alfred Kieser. 2011. "Fashion in Organization Theory: An Empirical Analysis of the Diffusion of Theoretical Concepts." Organization Studies 32: 655–81.

Bronfenbrenner, Martin. 1966. "Trends, Cycles, and Fads in Economic Writing." The American Economic Review 56: 538–52.

Brunsson, Nils. 1985. The Irrational Organization: Irrationality as a Basis for Organizational Action and Change. Chichester: John Wiley & Sons.

Brunsson, Nils. 1989. The Organization of Hypocrisy: Talk, Decisions and Actions in Organizations. Chichester: John Wiley & Sons.

Brunsson, Nils. 2007. "The Irrationality of Action and Action Rationality: Decisions, Ideologies, and Organizational Actions." In the Consequences of Decision-Making, edited by

Nils Brunsson, 32–49. Oxford, New York: Oxford University Press.

Burns, Tom, and George M. Stalker. 1961. The Management of Innovation. London: Tavistock.

Campbell, Andrew, and Michael Goold. 2000. The Collaborative Enterprise: Why Links Between Business Units Often Fail and How to Make Them Work. Cambridge: Perseus Books.

Carson, Paula P., Patricia A. Lanier, Kerry D. Carson, and Brandi N. Guidry. 2000. "Clearing a Path Through the Management Fashion Jungle: Some Preliminary Trailblazing." Academy of Management Journal 43: 1143–58.

Christensen, Clayton m 1998. The Innovator's Dilemma: When New Technologies Cause Great Firms to Fail. Boston: Harvard Business School Press.

Clark, Timothy, and David Greatbatch. 2016. "Management Fashion as Image-Spectacle." Management Communication Quarterly 17 (3): 396–424.

Clark, Timothy, and Graeme Salaman. 1996. "The Management Guru as Organizational Witchdoctor." Organization 3: 85–107.

Collins, David. 2000. Management Fads and Buzzwords: Critical-Practical Perspectives. London, New York: Routledge.

Collins, David. 2001a. "The Fad Motif in Management Scholarship." Employee Relations 23: 26–37. doi:https://doi.org/10.1108/01425450110366255.

Collins, David. 2020. Management Gurus: A Research Overview. London, New York: Routledge.

Collins, Jim. 2001b. Good to Great: Why Some Companies Make the Leap … And Others Don't. New York: HarperBusiness.

Crozier, Michel. 1989. L'entreprise à l'écoute: Apprendre le management postindustriel. Paris: Interéditions.

DiMaggio, Paul J. 2001. "Introduction: Making Sense of the Contemporary Firm and Prefiguring Its Future." In the Twenty-First-Century Firm: Changing Economic Organization in International Perspective, edited by Paul J. DiMaggio, 3–30. Princeton, Oxford: Princeton University Press.

DiMaggio, Paul J., and Walter W. Powell. 1983. "The Iron Cage Revisited: Institutional Isomorphism and Collective Rationality in Organizational Fields." American Sociological Review 48 (2): 147–60.

Drucker, Peter F. 1954. The Practice of Management. New York: Harper & Row.

Drucker, Peter F. 2016. People and Performance: The Best of Peter Drucker on Management. London: Taylor & Francis.

Ellis, Jonathan, and René J. Tissen. 2003. The Seven Deadly Sins of Management: How to Be a Virtuous Manager. London: Profile.

Esposito, Elena. 2004. Die Verbindlichkeit des Vorübergehenden: Paradoxien der Mode. Frankfurt a.M. Suhrkamp.

Feyerabend, Paul K. 1975. Against Method: Outline of an Anarchistic Theory of Knowledge. London: Verso.

Feyerabend, Paul K.1978. Science in a Free Society. London: Verso.

Fleck, Ludwik. 1935. Entstehung und Entwicklung einer wissenschaftlichen Tatsache. Basel: Benno Schwabe & Co.

Furnham, Adrian. 2004. Management and Myths: Challenging Business Fads, Fallacies and Fashions. London: Palgrave Macmillan.

Gill, John, and Sue Whittle. 1992. "Management by Panacea: Accounting for Transience." Journal of Management Studies 30: 281–95.

Glaser, Stan. 1997. "Management Duckspeak." Management Decision 35 (9): 653–55.

Greatbatch, David, and Timothy Clark. 2005. Management Speak: Why We Listen to What Management Gurus Tell Us. Online-Ausg. London: Routledge.

Grove, Andrew S. 1983. High Output Management. New York: Random House.

Guest, David. 1994. "Right Enough to Be Dangerously Wrong: An Analysis of the in Search of Excellence Phenomenon." In Human Resource Strategies, edited by Graeme Salaman. Reprinted., 5–19. London: Publ. in assoc. with the Open Univ. Sage.

Guillén, Mauro F. 1994. Models of Management: Work, Authority and Organization in a Comparative Perspective. Chicago, London: Chicago University Press.

Gulick, Luther. 1937. "Notes on the Theory of Organization." In Papers on the Science of Administration, edited by Luther Gulick and Lyndall F. Urwick, 1–46. New York: Columbia University Institute of Public Administration.

Hamel, Gary, and Michele Zanini. 2020. Humanocracy: Creating Organizations as Amazing as the People Inside Them. Boston Massachusetts: Harvard Business Review Press.

Hammer, Michael, and James Champy. 1993. Reengineering the Corporation: A Manifesto for Business Revolution. New York: HarperBusiness.

Hersey, Paul, and Kenneth H. Blanchard. 1969. "Managing Research and Development Personnel: An Application of Leadership Theory." Research Management 12: 331–38.

Hilmer, Frederick G., and Lex Donaldson. 1996. Management Redeemed: Debunking the Fads That Undermine Corporate Performance. New York: Free Press.

Höhn, Reinhard. 1966. Führungsbrevier der Wirtschaft. Bad Harzburg: Verlag für Wissenschaft, Wirtschaft und Technik.

Hsieh, Tony. 2010. Delivering Happiness: A Path to Profits, Passion, and Purpose. First edition. New York, Boston: Grand Central Publishing.

Huczynski, Andrzej. 1993a. "Explaining the Succession of Management Fads." The International Journal of Human Resource Management 4: 443–63.

Huczynski, Andrzej. 1993b. Management Gurus: What Makes Them and How to Become One. London: Routledge.

Huczynski, Andrzej. 2006. Management Gurus: What Makes Them and How to Become One. 2nd ed. London: Routledge.

Iacocca, Lee. 2007. Where Have All the Leaders Gone? New York: Scribner.

Ishikawa, Kaoru. 1987. What Is Total Quality Control? The Japanese Way. 6th ed. Englewood Cliffs: Prentice-Hall.

Jackson, Brad. 2001. Management Gurus and Management Fashions: A Dramatistic Inquiry. London, New York: Routledge.

Kanter, Rosabeth M. 1983. The Change Masters: Innovation for Productivity in the American Corporation. New York: Simon & Schuster.

Kieser, Alfred. 1996. "Moden & Mythen des Organisierens." Die Betriebswirtschaft 56: 21–39.

Kieser, Alfred. 1997a. "Moden & Mythen des Theoretisierens über die Organisation." In Individualisierung als Paradigma: Festschrift für Hans Jürgen Drumm, edited by Christian Scholz, 237–59. Stuttgart: Kohlhammer.

Kieser, Alfred. 1997b. "Rhetoric and Myth in Management Fashion." Organization 4: 49–74.

Kotter, John P. 2014. Accelerate: Building Strategic Agility for a Faster-Moving World. Boston: Harvard Business Review Press.

Kramer, Hugh E. 1975. "The Philosophical Foundation of Management Rediscovered." Management International Review 15 (2/3): 47–54.

Kühl, Stefan. 2015. Sisyphos im Management: Die vergebliche Suche nach der optimalen Organisationsstruktur. 2nd ed. Frankfurt a.M., New York: Campus.

Kühl, Stefan. 2017. Lateral Leading: A Very Brief Introduction to Power, Understanding and Trust. Princeton, Hamburg, Shanghai, Singapore, Versailles, Zurich: Organizational Dialogue Press.

Kühl, Stefan. 2020. Sisyphus in Management: The Futile Search for the Optimal Organizational Structure. Princeton, Hamburg, Shanghai, Singapore, Versailles, Zurich: Organizational Dialogue Press.

Kühl, Stefan. 2021. Organizations: A Short Introduction. Princeton, Hamburg, Shanghai, Singapore, Versailles, Zurich: Organizational Dialogue Press.

Kühl, Stefan. 2022. Useful Illegality: The Benefits of Breaking the Rules in Organizations. Princeton, Hamburg, Shanghai, Singapore, Versailles, Zurich: Organizational Dialogue Press.

Kühl, Stefan. 2023. Shadow Organizations: Agile Management and Unwanted Bureaucratization. Princeton, Hamburg, Shanghai, Singapore, Versailles, Zurich: Organizational Dialogue Press.

Kuhn, Thomas S. 1962. The Structure of Scientific Revolutions. Chicago: University of Chicago Press.

Laloux, Frederic. 2014. Reinventing Organizations: A Guide to Creating Organizations Inspired by the Next Stage of Human Consciousness. Brussels: Nelson Parker.

Laloux, Frederic. 2015. Reinventing Organizations: Ein Leifaden zur Gestaltung sinnstiftender Formen der Zusammenarbeit. München: Vahlen.

Lammers, Cornelis J. 1987. "Transcience and Persistence of Ideal Types in Organization Theory." In Research in the Sociology of Organizations, edited by Bacharach, Samuel B., DiTomaso, Nancy, 203–24. Greenwich: JAI Press.

Landier, Hubert. 1987. L'entreprise Polycellulaire: Pour Penser L'entreprise De Demain. Paris: Éditions Entreprise moderne.

Landier, Hubert. 1991. Vers l'entreprise intelligente: Dynamique du changement et mutation du management. Paris: Calmann Lévy.

Likert, Rensis, and Charles T. Araki. 1986. "Managing Without a Boss: System 5." Leadership and Organization Development Journal 7: 17–20.

Lowe, John W. G., and Elizabeth D. Lowe. 1982. "Cultural Pattern and Process: A Study of Stylistic Change in Women's Dress." American Anthropologist 84: 521–44.

Luhmann, Niklas. 1964. Funktionen und Folgen formaler Organisation. Berlin: Duncker & Humblot.

Luhmann, Niklas. 1970. Allgemeines Modell Organisierter Sozialsysteme. Bielefeld: Unveröff Ms.

Luhmann, Niklas. 1971. "Reform des öffentlichen Dienstes." In Politische Planung, edited by Niklas Luhmann, 203–56. Opladen: WDV.

Luhmann, Niklas. 1972. Rechtssoziologie. Reinbek: Rowohlt.

Luhmann, Niklas. 1973. Zweckbegriff und Systemrationalität. Frankfurt a.M. Suhrkamp.

Luhmann, Niklas. 1975. "Interaktion, Organisation, Gesell-schaft." In Soziologische Aufklärung 2, edited by Niklas Luh-mann, 9–20. Opladen: WDV.

Luhmann, Niklas. 1993. "Die Paradoxie des Entscheidens." Ver-waltungsarchiv 84: 287–310.

Luhmann, Niklas. 2000. Organisation und Entscheidung. Op-laden: WDV.

Mangham, I.L. 1990. "Management as Performing Art." British Journal of Management 1: 105–15.

March, James G. 1991. "Exploration and Exploitation in Orga-nizational Learning." Organization Science 2: 71–87.

March, James G. 2010. The Ambiguities of Experience. Ithaca: Cornell University Press.

Mayo, Elton. 1933. The Human Problems of an Industrial Civi-lization. New York: Macmillan.

Meyer, John W., and Brian Rowan. 1977. "Institutionalized Or-ganizations. Formal Structure as Myth and Ceremony." Amer-ican Journal of Sociology 83 (2): 340–63.

Micklethwait, John, and Adrian Wooldrige. 1996. The Witch Doctors: Making Sense of the Management Gurus. London: William Heinemann.

Miller, Danny, and Jon Hartwick. 2002. "Spotting Management Fads." Harvard Business Review 80 (10): 26–27.

Miller, Danny, Jon Hartwick, and Isabelle Le Breton-Miller. 2004. "How to Detect a Management Fad—And Distinguish It from a Classic." Business Horizons 47 (4): 7–16.

Neuberger, Oswald. 1994. "Zur Ästhetisierung des Manage-ments." In Managementforschung 4, edited by Georg Schreyögg and Peter Conrad, 1–70. Berlin, New York: Walter de Gruyter.

Neuberger, Oswald. 1996. "Im Anderen das Eigene bekämpfen." Die Betriebswirtschaft 56: 276–78.

Odiorne, George S. 1965. Management by Objectives: A System of Managerial Leadership. New York: Pitman.

Örtenblad, Anders, ed. 2015. Handbook of Research on Man-agement Ideas and Panaceas: Adaptation and Context.

Cheltenham, Northampton: Edward Elgar. http://www.elgar-online.com/view/9781783475599.xml.

Örtenblad, Anders, Peter Lamb, and Shih-wei Hsu. 2015. "Empowering Students to Translate Management Panaceas." In Örtenblad 2015, 380–96.

Ostroff, Frank. 1999. The Horizontal Organization: What the Organization of the Future Looks Like and How It Delivers Value to Customers. New York: Oxford University Press.

Pascale, Richard T. 1990. Managing on the Edge: How the Smartest Companies Use Conflict to Stay Ahead. New York.

Peters, Thomas J. 1988. Thriving on Chaos: Handbook for a Management Revolution. New York: Harper & Row.

Peters, Thomas J. 1992. Liberation Management: Necessary Disorganization for the Nanosecond Nineties. New York: Knopf.

Peters, Thomas J., and Robert H. Waterman. 1982. In Search of Excellence: Lessons from America's Best-Run Companies. New York: Harper & Row.

Pfeffer, Jeffrey, and Robert I. Sutton. 2006. Hard Facts, Dangerous Half-Truths, and Total Nonsense: Profiting from Evidence-Based Management. Boston MA: Harvard Business School Press.

Pinchot, Gifford. 1988. Intrapreneuring: Mitarbeiter als Unternehmer. Wiesbaden: Gabler.

Porter, Michael E. 1980. Competitive Strategy: Techniques for Analyzing Industries and Competitors. New York: Free Press.

Purser, Ronald E., and Steven Cabana. 1998. The Self Managing Organization: How Leading Companies Are Transforming the Work of Teams for Real Impact. New York: Free Press.

Reay, Trish, Samia Chreim, Karen Golden-Biddle, Elizabeth Goodrick, B. E. Williams, Ann Casebeer, Amy Pablo, and C. R. Hinings. 2013. "Transforming New Ideas into Practice: An Activity Based Perspective on the Institutionalization of Practices." Journal of Management Studies 50: 963–90.

Robertson, Brian J. 2015. Holacracy: The Revolutionary Management System That Abolishes Hierarchy. London: Portfolio Penguin.

Robertson, Brian J. 2016. Holacracy: Ein Revolutionäres Management-System für eine volatile Welt. München: Verlag Franz Vahlen.

Rodríguez, Darío. 1991. Gestion organizacional: Elementos para su estudio. Santiago de Chile: Pontificia Universidad Católica de Chile.

Roethlisberger, Fritz J., and William J. Dickson. 1939. Management and the Worker: An Account of a Research Program Conducted by the Western Electric Company, Hawthorne Works, Chicago. Cambridge: Harvard University Press.

Scharmer, Otto. 2007. "Theorie U: Von der Zukunft her führen: Presencing als evolutionäre Grammatik und soziale Technik für die Erschliessung des vierten Feldes sozialen Werdens." Gesprächspsychotherapie und Personzentrierte Beratung 4: 202–11.

Scharmer, Otto. 2009a. Theorie U: Von der Zukunft her führen; Presencing als soziale Technik. Heidelberg: Carl-Auer.

Scharmer, Otto. 2009b. Theory U: Leading from the Future as It Emerges. San Francisco, London: Berrett-Koehler; McGraw-Hill.

Schumpeter, Joseph A. 1947. Kapitalismus, Sozialismus Und Demokratie. Tübingen: J. C. B. Mohr.

Senge, Peter M. 1990. The Fifth Discipline: The Art and Practice of the Learning Organization. New York: Doubleday.

Simmel, Georg. 2012. "Philosophie der Mode." In Georg Simmel. Gesamtausgabe: Band 10, edited by Otthein Rammstedt, 8–37. Frankfurt a.M. Suhrkamp.

Simon, Herbert A. 1946. "The Proverbs of Administration." Public Administration Review 6: 53–67.

Sorge, Arndt, and Arjen van Witteloostuijn. 2004. "The (Non) Sense of Organizational Change: An Essai About Universal Management Hypes, Sick Consultancy Metaphors, and Healthy Organization Theories." Organization Studies 25: 1205–31.

Spyridonidis, Dimitrios, Graeme Currie, Stefan Heusinkveld, Karoline Strauss, and Andrew Sturdy. 2016. "The Translation of Management Knowledge: Challenges, Contributions and

New Directions." International Journal of Management Reviews 18: 231–35.

Starbuck, William H. 2009. "The Constant Causes of Never-Ending Faddishness in the Behavioral and Social Sciences." Scandinavian Journal of Management 25: 108–16.

Sturdy, Andrew, Stefan Heusinkveld, Trish Reay, and David Strang. 2019. "Researching Management Ideas: An Introduction." In the Oxford Handbook of Management Ideas, edited by Andrew Sturdy, Stefan Heusinkveld, Trish Reay, and David Strang, 1–23. Oxford: Oxford University Press.

Sunstein, Cass R. 2001. "Academic Fads and Fashions (With Special Reference to Law)." Michigan Law Review 99: 1251–64.

Taylor, Frederick W. 1967. The Principles of Scientific Management. London: Norton.

Thompson, James D. 1967. Organizations in Action. New York: McGraw-Hill.

Tichy, Noel M. 1995. Regieanweisung für Revolutionäre: Unternehmenswandel in drei Akten. Frankfurt a.M., New York: Campus.

Toffler, Alvin. 1971. Future Shock. New York: Bantam Book.

Turco, Catherine J. 2016. The Conversational Firm: Rethinking Bureaucracy in the Age of Social Media. New York: Columbia University Press.

Wendler, Roy. 2012. "The Maturity of Maturity Model Research: A Systematic Mapping Study." Information and Software Technology 54: 1317–39.

Whyte, William F. 1951. "Small Groups and Large Organizations." In Social Psychology at the Crossroads, edited by John R. Rohrer and Muzafer Sherif, 297–312. New York: Harper.

Womack, James P., Daniel T. Jones, and Daniel Roos. 1990. The Machine That Changed the World. New York: Maxwell Macmillan International.

The manufacturer's authorised representative in the EU is Springer
Nature Customer Service Centre GmbH, Europaplatz 3, 69115 Heidelberg,
Germany. If you have any concerns regarding our products, please
contact ProductSafety@springernature.com

Printed and bound by CPI Group (UK) Ltd, Croydon, CR0 4YY
23/04/2026
02095597-0001